Support for living?

This publication can be provided in other formats,
such as large print, Braille and audio.
Please contact:
Communications, Joseph Rowntree Foundation,
The Homestead, 40 Water End, York YO30 6WP.
Tel: 01904 615905. Email: info@jrf.org.uk

✔ **Available in other formats**

Support for living?

The impact of the Supporting People programme on housing and support for adults with learning disabilities

Rachel Fyson, Beth Tarleton and Linda Ward

JOSEPH ROWNTREE
FOUNDATION

First published in Great Britain in 2007 by

The Policy Press
Fourth Floor, Beacon House
Queen's Road
Bristol BS8 1QU
UK

Tel no   +44 (0)117 331 4054
Fax no   +44 (0)117 331 4093
Email   tpp-info@bristol.ac.uk
www.policypress.org.uk

Published for the Joseph Rowntree Foundation by The Policy Press

ISBN 978 1 84742 042 8

British Library Cataloguing in Publication Data
A catalogue record for this book is available from the British Library.

Library of Congress Cataloging-in-Publication Data
A catalog record for this book has been requested.

Rachel Fyson is a lecturer in social work at the University of Nottingham. **Beth Tarleton** is a research
fellow and **Linda Ward** is Professor of Disability and Social Policy, both at the Norah Fry Research Centre,
University of Bristol.

The **Joseph Rowntree Foundation** has supported this project as part of its programme of research and
innovative development projects, which it hopes will be of value to policy makers, practitioners and service
users. The facts presented and views expressed in this report are, however, those of the authors and not
necessarily those of the Foundation.

Cover illustration by Angela Martin
Cover design by Qube Design Associates, Bristol
Printed in Great Britain by Latimer Trend, Plymouth

Contents

List of tables and figures

Tables

Figure

Acknowledgements

We are grateful to the Joseph Rowntree Foundation for funding this study, and to Chrysa Apps and Alison Jarvis at the Foundation for their advice and support. Our thanks also to the members of the project's advisory group for their help, constructive comments and enthusiasm along the way – David Congdon, Mencap; David Heather, Places for People; David Williams, Ability Housing; Nicholas Pleace, The Centre for Housing Policy, University of York; Nick Sweet, National Housing Federation; and John Kennedy at the Joseph Rowntree Foundation.

The project would not have been possible without the enormous amount of help from all those who agreed to be interviewed for the project: tenants, frontline staff, managers, Supporting People team members, other professionals and service providers and commissioners. A big thank you to them for allowing us into their homes, lives and offices, and for being so honest about the issues and difficulties they faced, as well as their positive stories. Thanks also to members of Supporting People teams across the country who responded so helpfully to our request for copies of their five-year plans.

Thanks also to Steve Strong, a member of the Valuing People Support Team at the time of the study, Carl Poll (previously director of KeyRing), Paul Watson at Hanover Housing Association and Maurice Harker at Housing Options for sharing ideas and signposting us to helpful sources of information at the start of the project.

Finally, we are grateful to colleagues at the Norah Fry Research Centre, University of Bristol for their help: Maggi Walton, for administrative and other support throughout the project and Sammantha Cave, for help in preparing the final report for publication.

Summary

Background

The Supporting People programme, which went live on 1 April 2003, was designed to separate out the costs of bricks-and-mortar housing (which, where needed, would continue to be paid through Housing Benefit) from the costs of the support necessary to enable vulnerable adults to attain or maintain independent tenancies. For people with learning disabilities, this new funding mechanism appeared to offer a much-needed opportunity for some of the changes set out in the 2001 *Valuing People* White Paper (DH, 2001) to be made a reality.

This study set out to examine how local Supporting People teams were interpreting national guidelines in relation to the provision of housing-related support and to explore the impact that this was having on housing and support for people with learning disabilities. We were also keen to discover the extent to which the *Valuing People* core aims – of promoting rights, choice, independence and control in the lives of people with learning disabilities – were being supported by this new programme.

Methods

Four geographically and socially diverse administering authorities were selected as the location for detailed qualitative research, involving interviews with 31 people with learning disabilities, 11 support workers, 10 managers of support provider organisations, 4 members of local Supporting People teams; and 10 managers and/or commissioners from across housing, social services and health. Five-year Supporting People strategies from across England were also analysed.

Results

Defining 'housing-related support'

The government has not issued authoritative guidance on how 'housing-related support' should be defined and this has led to wide variations in operational definitions at local level. The consequence of this for people with learning disabilities has been significant differences between authorities in relation to the availability of Supporting People funding. Since Supporting People operates within a strictly cash-limited budget, authorities in our study had chosen to restrict the cost of individual support packages by one or more of the following means:

- limiting support to a defined list of 'eligible support tasks';
- capping the number of support hours per person per week (limits ranged from 10 to 30 hours);
- limiting the cost they were willing to pay per hour of support (limits ranged from £12.05 to £22.00 per hour);
- capping the cost of support per person per week (limits ranged from £200 to £500+ per week).

All of these limits, to a greater or lesser extent, restricted the availability of Supporting People services for people with learning disabilities. Some local Supporting People teams were willing to consider developing individual support packages that included elements of both housing-related support and further hours of care – funded from either social service or health budgets. Others, however, argued that Supporting People monies should be used exclusively for individuals who did not attract a statutory duty of care under the 1948 National Assistance Act (that is, were not eligible for support from either health or social services). In the latter areas, the availability of Supporting People monies was, to all intents and purposes, thereby limited to people with learning disabilities who had low support needs.

Outcomes for service users

The housing and support of people with learning disabilities who received Supporting People funds varied considerably according not only to the amount of support they received, but also to the structure of their housing and support services. The two key dimensions of difference were, first, whether people lived alone (individual tenancies) or with others (shared tenancies) and, second, whether they received floating support (staff visiting their homes to help with specific tasks) or accommodation-based support (staff teams based in tenants' homes). In practice, these dimensions of difference were not independent of one another: shared tenancies were associated with accommodation-based support and individual tenancies were associated with floating support.

The advantages and disadvantages of these different ways of providing housing and support can be summarised as follows:

Shared tenancies with accommodation–based support	Individual tenancies with floating support
Danger of less individualised support	Fully individual support
24-hour staff cover sometimes possible	Limited number of support hours available each day
Maximum flexibility of support, as staff are always at hand	Difficult to change support hours at short notice
Less privacy/time alone	More privacy/time alone
Less chance of being lonely	More chance of being lonely
Support and housing often managed by the same organisation	Clear separation between landlord and support provider
Possibility of minimising costs per hour of support	Potentially higher costs per hour of support, because of the need to allow for staff travel time
System suited to the employment of full-time staff – giving greater consistency of support	System suited to the employment of part-time staff – giving less consistency of support

Although all services funded by Supporting People necessarily defined themselves as supported living services, it was difficult to identify how some of the shared tenancy arrangements differed from high-quality, small-scale registered care homes. This was particularly the case where some of the basic principles of supported living appeared to be being overlooked – including having staff offices within people's homes; staff routinely holding (and using) front door keys; and staff hours of work based on a set pattern of shifts.

Choice, control and independence

The lives and lifestyles of individual service users varied according to the extent to which support providers had taken on board the principles and practice of enabling tenants with learning disabilities to exert choice, control and independence. All the tenants we interviewed were supported to make choices about everyday activities – such as what to wear, what to eat or what to do. However, there were many important decisions that typically remained under the control of service managers and/or commissioners – including where individuals lived, who they lived with, and who provided their support.

Both the tenants and the support staff whom we interviewed tended to talk mostly in terms of 'choice' and 'control'. By contrast, managers and commissioners were more likely to focus on promoting 'independence'. However, there was no agreement about what 'independence' might constitute for a person with a learning disability. Paid support staff were frequently the main – or only – source of social contact for tenants living alone. A minority of managers and commissioners wished to place greater emphasis on developing interdependence between tenants and their local community, but successes in this area were few and social networks were heavily dependent on the involvement of family members. Part of the reason for this is that local Supporting People guidelines typically preclude money being used to provide support for either social or employment-related activities. As a consequence, tenants with learning disabilities could find themselves well supported in practical aspects of day-to-day life (self-care, cooking, housework and so on), but socially isolated. A number of people with individual tenancies explicitly talked about being lonely. Difficulties in achieving social integration were often exacerbated (particularly in urban areas) by bullying and abuse from neighbours and other members of the public.

Five-year Supporting People strategies

Key points that emerged from our analysis of these strategies were that:

- only 5% of authorities had produced a version of their strategy in a format that was accessible to people with learning disabilities;
- average costs per person per year for people with learning disabilities were roughly twice the overall average cost for all service user groups;
- the proportion of local budget spent on services for people with learning disabilities varied hugely: 6% of authorities spent 10% or less on people with learning disabilities, while 11% spent 40% or more on this group of service users;
- administering authorities indicate that they plan in the future to focus on the development of services to people with learning disabilities that offer individual tenancies with low-level floating support.

Conclusion

The impact of Supporting People on housing and support for people with learning disabilities has been mixed. On the plus side, the programme has provided a much-needed injection of cash into services for people with learning disabilities, which has enabled the development of an increasing number of supported living services. Importantly, the tenants of these services typically expressed pleasure with their homes and with the support they received. Despite variations in the way in which both housing and support were provided by different supported living services, there was a consensus among tenants that such services offered them a significant degree of choice and control, particularly in relation to day-to-day decisions.

Against this must be balanced the evidence that most important decisions continue to be made by service managers and commissioners. Worryingly, there were also indications that the rapid expansion of self-styled supported living schemes, following the sudden availability of Supporting People monies, may have diluted the meaning of 'supported living'. Schemes based on shared tenancies with accommodation-based support were sometimes little different from the registered care homes they had replaced. This was particularly true where services ignored some of the key legal and ideological differences between supported living and care homes – for example, the importance of tenancy rights; the belief that staff should not have offices in people's homes; the belief that tenants should control access to their own homes. Moreover, although services funded by Supporting People offer people with learning disabilities the prospect of geographical integration, this research highlighted the continuing failure of most service providers to adequately support the social integration of people with learning disabilities within their local communities.

Introduction

Over the last decade the favoured model for providing housing and support to people with learning disabilities has become what is variously called 'supported housing' , or 'independent' or 'supported' 'living' (Gillinson et al, 2005). 'Supported living' assumes that people with learning disabilities, like other adult members of society, should be free to choose where and with whom they live; and that the support services they need, to enable them to live as independently as possible, should be provided to them *in their own homes* (Kinsella, 1993; Simons, 1995; Simons and Ward, 1997).

This study was premised on a belief that supported living, as a framework for providing housing and support, can enable people with learning disabilities to have more control over their daily lives. In 2003, funding for this type of support was rationalised through the introduction of the Supporting People programme. Supporting People is a government programme that aims to offer improved ways of providing housing-related support to people who need help to retain their housing tenancies and attain or maintain independence. Such funding might enable more people with learning disabilities to enjoy the benefits of supported living. It was, however, recognised that there were likely to be some difficulties with the way in which the Supporting People programme was being implemented in relation to people with learning disabilities, which the research could document.

The values that underpin supported living were not under question in this study. Rather, the questions explored by this research were about whether the Supporting People programme can deliver effective supported living schemes. Can it, for example, offer a better framework for supporting people with learning disabilities than is available within registered residential care homes – currently the most common means of providing housing and support to this group of people?

We hope that by posing some important questions raised in the early stages of the Supporting People programme, this report may encourage professionals involved in providing and delivering supported living to think how the services they offer might be improved and how tenants with learning disabilities can be supported to safely maximise their independence.

Housing and people with learning disabilities

As recently as 50 years ago, most adults with learning disabilities and their families in the UK were faced with a stark choice in terms of housing and support: either remain living in the family home – with little or no assistance from statutory services – or move into the institutional surroundings of a long-stay 'mental handicap' hospital. Much has changed in the lives of people with learning disabilities over the intervening half century (Atkinson, 1997; Rolph et al, 2005). The preferred model of housing and support for people with learning disabilities over this period (as expressed through government policy) has shifted from hospital wards, through hostel accommodation to registered care homes, small group homes and individual tenancies.

The changes that have come about in the housing and support available to people with learning disabilities have, in part, been a reflection of both changes in government policy and the availability of funding. Change has also, increasingly, been driven by the demands of people with learning disabilities, their families and supporters, who have campaigned at local and national level for the housing and support they want and need. However, despite many individual success stories, there remains clear evidence that a very significant proportion of people with learning disabilities still do not have any control over where, and with whom, they live (Gorfin and McGlaughlin, 2003).

Although the overall direction of change has been positive, with relatively few people now remaining in hospitals (239 people with learning disabilities remained in long-stay hospital by the summer of 2006; reported by Hunter, 2006), and increasing numbers in supported housing, national policy has not always moved smoothly or consistently in the direction of improved choice in housing and support for people with learning disabilities.

The origins and growth of the 'supported living' movement

Supported living initially emerged from within the disability rights movement (Gillinson et al, 2005), and is now widely recognised as one of the most important means by which disabled people (including those with learning disabilities) can be empowered to have more control of their lives. Key principles are that people's housing needs should be assessed, and met, separately from their needs for support, and that they are enabled to be in control of their own lives as far as possible and supported to be fully engaged – both geographically and socially – within their local community (Simons, 1998, 2000).

What is supported living?

A provisional list of the attributes of supported living, as drafted by the Association for Supported Living (www.associationsupportedliving.org/aboutUs.php) in 2004 states:

- The tenant should have been offered a range of options for their living arrangements.
- The tenant should have real choice in who provides their support.
- There should be clear separation between the provider of support and the provider of accommodation.
- The tenant should have a tenancy agreement.
- There should be no contract between the provider of support and the provider of the property.
- The tenancy agreement should make no mention of support provision.
- The tenant should have a choice in where they live.
- The tenant should have a choice about with whom they live.
- There should not be an office for use by support staff in the property.
- The tenant should decide who enters their home.

Standards in supported living (Paradigm, 2002)

- I choose who I live with.
- I choose where I live.
- I choose who supports me.
- I choose how I am supported.
- I choose what happens in my own home.
- I have my own home.
- I make friendships and relationships with people on my terms.
- I am supported to be safe and healthy on my terms.
- I have the same rights and responsibilities as other citizens.

These principles of supported living are based on a set of values that recognise the rights, and responsibilities, of people with learning disabilities to exercise some control over how they live. It is largely the presence of these values, allied with a person-centred approach to delivering housing and support, that differentiates supported living from other ways of providing housing and support services.

The Valuing People *White Paper*

The *Valuing People* White Paper is about promoting the rights, choice, independence and inclusion of people with learning disabilities. Its publication in 2001 (DH, 2001) marked the government's recognition that housing and support are crucial to enabling people with learning disabilities to have choice and more control of their lives. Although the White Paper noted that supported living was "associated with people having greater overall choice and a wider range of community activities" (DH, 2001, p 73), it did not explicitly promote supported living as a preferred option. Instead, it outlined a number of possible models of housing provision, including supported living, small-scale ordinary housing and intentional communities (where people with learning disabilities live alongside others in an intentionally created community with shared goals).

The Supporting People programme (then being shadowed by local authorities prior to full implementation) was mentioned in *Valuing People* as a future source of funding that would enable local authorities to offer greater flexibility in their provision of housing and support to people with learning disabilities. Supporting People, it was also hoped, would promote more effective joint working between health, housing and social services, as the divisions between services had long been recognised as contributing to poor outcomes for people with learning disabilities (Arblaster et al, 1996, 1998; DH, 1999).

Since the publication of *Valuing People*, much effort has gone into promoting further change in services for people with learning disabilities (Fyson and Ward, 2004), but progress has been constrained by limited availability of resources. As a result, unmet need in relation to housing and support remains high, with a recent national survey indicating that 62% of people with learning disabilities aged 16 and over still live with their families (Emerson et al, 2005). At the same time, progress reports on the implementation of *Valuing People* continue to highlight the importance of housing (Valuing People Support Team, 2005; HM Government, 2005). Effective and efficient use of the resources available through Supporting People provides one means of giving a greater number of people with learning disabilities the housing support that they want and need in order to live more independently.

The Supporting People programme

A lengthy run-in period preceded full implementation of Supporting People (on 1 April 2003), during which time local authorities had sought to identify and rationalise the complex funding streams through which various vulnerable groups received housing-related support (Griffiths, 2000). The programme was intended to help *all* people who might need support in relation to their housing, and launch documents included the following statements:

> This is an opportunity to enhance provision, building on excellent good practice locally. Supporting People breaks the link between support and tenure. It will encompass previously marginalised and excluded groups and provides a flexible approach to the delivery of support. (DETR, 2001, p 107)

> Alongside mainstream health and social services expenditure on care and support for people with learning disabilities, Supporting People will have much to contribute to diversification of opportunities and enhancing the quality of support for people with learning disabilities living in the community. (DETR, 2001, p 41)

From the outset, then, people with learning disabilities were included within the remit of the Supporting People programme alongside other groups of potentially vulnerable people. Although the scope of the programme has since been defined more closely, people with learning disabilities still remain among those identified as eligible for housing-related support as the listing of potential recipients from the Office of the Deputy Prime Minister (ODPM) (ODPM, 2004a, p 2) makes clear:

- People who have been homeless or a rough sleeper
- Ex-offenders and people at risk of offending and imprisonment
- People with a physical or sensory disability
- People at risk of domestic violence
- People with alcohol and drug problems
- Elderly people
- Young people at risk
- People with HIV and AIDS
- People with learning difficulties
- Travellers
- Homeless families with support needs

As well as seeking to offer more effective support to vulnerable groups, the Supporting People programme was underpinned by a desire on the part of government to separate out 'bricks and mortar' housing costs, which would continue to be paid as rent (and through Housing Benefit, where individuals were eligible for this) from the costs of housing-related support. Although a broad range of housing-related support services could be funded through Supporting People, there were also some clear exclusions. Most significantly, for people with learning disabilities, Supporting People monies could *not* be used to pay for housing-related support provided in the context of registered residential care. Rather, this was money that was available to people with learning disabilities living in *supported housing* – individuals who held their own tenancies, but required support to enable them to live there. It is also worth noting that this money could not be used to fund services to meet people's employment or social support needs.

The political backdrop: charges of cost-shunting

In the run-up to the full implementation of Supporting People it appeared that some local authorities were attempting to shift costs away from overstretched social services community care budgets and into Supporting People by the simple means of deregistering existing residential care homes for people with learning disabilities and renaming them 'supported living services'. If done in good faith, that is, to enhance the choice, independence and social inclusion of people with learning disabilities, such moves were arguably entirely within the spirit of both Supporting People and *Valuing People*.

Nevertheless, as costs rose, concern was expressed (*The Guardian*, 2003) that, in some cases, deregistration was merely a paper exercise, with residents not experiencing any significant changes to their independence or the right to make choices. It was also argued that such deregistrations potentially placed people with learning disabilities at an increased risk of abuse, since (unlike registered care homes) supported living services did not come under the regulatory framework and protective procedures of the Commission for Social Care Inspection (formerly the Care Standards Commission) (Simons, 2001). Specifically, under Section 3 of the 2000 Care Standards Act, an establishment is a care home if it provides accommodation *together with* nursing or personal care – the very scenario that Supporting People was designed to prevent, since housing and support needs are assessed and funded independently of one another.

Supporting People became an important item on the political agenda because of concerns over exponential increases in the overall cost of the programme. Following fears during the run-up to implementation that take-up of the new funding stream would be low, there was a late surge of projects applying for funding. With the initial budget uncapped, this led to a very significant uplift in overall costs over a very short period of time. As a consequence, a review of the Supporting People programme was launched in order to examine both the extent to which Supporting People services had been cost-shunted from other budgets and whether schemes funded under Supporting People were complying with grant conditions. Contemporary reports in national newspapers suggested that services for people with learning disabilities were likely to be targeted if the review indicated that cuts would be made to the Supporting People budget.

> Originally Supporting People was meant to pay for relatively low-level care of groups such as rough sleepers, frail older people and women fleeing domestic violence. It was estimated to cost £750m at most, but that has now ballooned by more than £1bn – partly because the programme is being used, some say, to pay for intensive support, such as care for people with learning disabilities. (*The Guardian*, 2003)

What the newspapers failed to acknowledge was the inevitability of services for people with learning disabilities taking a large slice of the Supporting People budgets. This was not necessarily linked to cost-shunting or the provision of high levels of support, but simply a reflection of two facts: first, the high level of unmet need for housing-related support among this group of people, and second the fact that – unlike other potential service user groups – people with learning disabilities are likely to require lifelong, rather than short-term, support.

In the event, the independent review of the Supporting People programme (Robson Rhodes, 2004) did not single out services for people with learning disabilities in the manner predicted by some. The review acknowledged that some cost inflation and some cost-shunting had occurred during the run-up to full implementation. It concluded that £1.8 billion was an excessive amount to pay for 'legacy provision', that is, existing services, and that efficiency savings needed to be made in order to enable the development of new services in the future. It also noted that Supporting People monies were distributed unevenly between authorities, and that this inequality needed to be rectified.

In relation to people with learning disabilities, the review noted that the philosophy of the Supporting People provision was in line with that of *Valuing People*, but commented that: "more needs to be done to establish a clearer national picture of the number of people with learning disabilities and their needs" (Robson Rhodes, 2004, p 29). It also acknowledged that "people with higher-level needs can require a multi-layered package of social care, health care and housing related support" (Robson Rhodes, 2004, p 30). However, although the report recognised that there remained "a level of unmet need" among both people with learning disabilities and other client groups, it concluded that this need could be met by the judicious financial management of existing resources.

Following the Robson Rhodes review, in September 2004 the ODPM published a further briefing paper (Matrix Research & Consultancy, 2004), which set out proposals for developing a distribution formula for Supporting People monies. The aim was to reduce inequities between administering authorities ('administering authorities' is a generic term for the various types of local government authorities responsible for administering Supporting People monies) and work towards a distribution of funds based on need, rather than legacy (existing service) provision. At the time the fieldwork for this research project was underway, this distribution formula had recently been published. Some administering authorities were looking forward to increases in their Supporting People budgets, while others were facing significant cuts.

The aims of the research study

Supporting People offered – and continues to offer – an opportunity for the development of housing-related support for people with learning disabilities that was truly person-centred and available for more than a lucky minority. This opportunity arose not only because the launch of the programme coincided with the ongoing implementation of the *Valuing People* White Paper (DH, 2001), but also because of the programme's own explicit emphasis on service user involvement (ODPM, 2004d, 2004e) – both in planning services and in being empowered to take control of their own lives through the provision of supported living services.

The overall aims of the study were:

- to examine how local administering authorities were interpreting Supporting People guidelines in relation to the provision of housing-related support services for people with learning disabilities;
- to examine the impact – if any – of the Supporting People programme on the lives of people with learning disabilities and on their housing and support services.

Supporting People is being implemented across England, Scotland and Wales. There are, however, significant differences in the programme of each country with regard to both financial systems and definitions of eligible support services (Watson et al, 2003). Furthermore, in relation to services specifically for people with learning disabilities, *Valuing People* applies only in England. For these reasons the research on which this report is based was undertaken solely in England.

Research methods

Four local authorities from different parts of England were approached to take part in the study. The authorities were selected partly on the basis of what was known about their early implementation of Supporting People: for example, it was possible to identify high and low spending authorities from figures published by the ODPM. Thus, one authority was included which was known to have a very high unit spend on Supporting People services for people with learning disabilities and another whose unit spend was in the lowest decile. Authorities were also chosen on the basis of exemplifying a range of different social, political and geographical features – they included inner-city, urban and rural areas; unitary and two-tier local authorities; and an authority with a significant population of people from minority ethnic communities.

Within each authority, semi-structured interviews were undertaken with the following groups of people:

- people with learning disabilities who were receiving services funded (at least in part) by Supporting People monies;
- frontline support staff – the people who provided direct support to tenants with learning disabilities;

- managers of housing support services – this included organisations from the statutory, voluntary and independent sectors
- members of Supporting People teams;
- managers and commissioners from within statutory specialist learning disability services, including both health and social services.

In total, 66 interviews were undertaken, as shown in Table A1 in the Appendix, where further details on the methods are given.

A review of five-year Supporting People plans, which the ODPM required each administering authority to produce by April 2005, was also undertaken in order to provide an insight into the likely future direction of service provision for people with learning disabilities. Further details are provided in the Appendix. The research interviews and documentary analysis took place between spring 2004 and summer 2005.

What people with learning disabilities think about supported living

From the perspective of the tenants involved in our study, the move to supported living was generally a positive one. Despite some problems, including loneliness and instances of bullying in the local community, every tenant we interviewed, with one exception, was pleased to be in their current home.

Just under half of the people with learning disabilities to whom we spoke had previously lived in some form of institutionalised setting; most of these had lived in residential care homes, but several people had also experienced life in hostel-type accommodation, while one person had spent time in a long-stay hospital. The remainder of the tenants had moved directly from their family home into supported living services. Those who had moved from their family home were as enthusiastic about their new homes as those who had moved from more institutionalised settings.

People who had previously lived in a hostel (with, say, 20 others) were particularly critical of their previous accommodation. Both the physical and social environments of hostels were disliked. Ex-residents described hostel premises as "too old and scruffy; they didn't clean the toilet properly" or as "a filthy, dreadful place. The bathroom and toilet stinked". These tenants had also disliked living in such large groups, saying, for example, that they "didn't like living on top of each other", with so many other people with such wide-ranging needs. They talked of how "there were people fighting with each other and people downstairs smoking" or described how other residents "used to shake". One said "I was sick of living there with old people and people who had nowhere to go".

All of the people quoted above had previously lived in relatively large-scale accommodation. It is possible, therefore, that some of the difficulties described were created in large part by the pressure of numbers. We did not come across anyone in the study who was able to describe to us, from their own experience, the similarities or differences between a previous life in a small residential group home (of, say, three to four residents) with a current situation where they lived with the same number of people, but in a supported living service.

To genuinely achieve the principles of supported living, housing schemes need to offer more than just an improvement on institutional care, however. Supported living does not measure itself against residential settings; its yardstick for comparison is ordinary people, in ordinary housing, living ordinary lives. Judged from this perspective, and based on the findings of this study, the impact of the Supporting People programme on the housing and support available to people with learning disabilities has been questionable, for the reasons that we will discuss in the chapters that follow.

Eligibility for Supporting People funding

Defining what constitutes 'housing-related support' is crucial for administering authorities as they implement their local Supporting People programmes. This chapter examines the various working definitions of housing-related support used in the administering authorities where the research was undertaken and the impact of different definitions on the availability of Supporting People funding for people with learning disabilities.

The working definition agreed by administering authorities is critical. The variation in definitions had an impact on both the *availability* of Supporting People funding for people with learning disabilities as well as the *scope* of work that could be undertaken with them under the eligibility criteria set by government. Where housing-related support was defined in very narrow terms it could preclude people with higher support needs from accessing Supporting People funding. Conversely, if housing-related support was defined very broadly, it could result in a small number of people receiving very intensive – and hence very expensive – packages of support, but others receiving no support at all, because there was no money left in the cash-limited pot.

The knock-on effect of different interpretations of government guidelines, then, has been to create variations in the availability of support for people with learning disabilities, depending on where they live.

What is 'housing-related support'?

Supporting People money is intended to pay for 'housing-related support'. But determining what does, or does not, come under the definition of housing-related support has proved far from simple. Just as arguments over the distinction between healthcare and social care emerged during the implementation of the 1990 NHS and Community Care Act (Means and Smith, 1994; Lewis and Glennerster, 1996), so difficulties are now emerging over how to distinguish housing-related support from social care. In both cases the need to draw the distinction arises because different types of care or support are funded from different budgets. In the case of Supporting People, this budget can only be used to pay for housing-related support; any input that is determined to be social care must be financed from alternative budgets, typically local authority community care money.

To put it another way, the distinction between housing-related support and social care is a bureaucratic construct. It is an artificial distinction, not originating from an absolute or objective difference between two genuinely separate 'categories' of care or support, but arising because of the need to have a functional means of deciding which budget should fund which services.

Bearing this in mind, the guidance issued by the ODPM in 2004 defined housing-related support in surprisingly broad terms:

The primary purpose of housing-related support is to develop and sustain an individual's capacity to live independently in their accommodation. Some examples of housing-related support services include enabling individuals to access their correct benefit entitlement, ensuring they have the correct skills to maintain a tenancy, advising on home improvements and accessing a community alarm service. Other services include a home visit for a short period each week or an on-site full-time support worker for a longer period of time. A range of services and activities can be tailored to an individual's specific needs. (ODPM, 2004a, p 2)

This wide-ranging definition had the advantage of not inadvertently excluding individuals whose particular support needs might not fit easily within more prescriptive criteria. However, since Supporting People is a cash-limited budget (that is, there is a fixed amount of money available each year, rather than the budget being determined by demand as is the case with some benefits) this creates a need to restrict eligibility in order to avoid overspending. Therefore, as a consequence of the lack of a sufficiently precise definition from central government, Supporting People teams in each administering authority have had to develop their own definitions of what does, or does not, constitute housing-related support.

Members of Supporting People teams were acutely aware that the government definition was insufficient for operational purposes:

'There's no legal definition at all. There is nothing that gives 100% clarification on what housing-related support actually is.'

'It is very difficult to define it [housing-related support] as an absolute, because the government itself I don't think has come up with an absolute definition.'

Interviewees from Supporting People teams often cited very broad 'rules of thumb' as the basis for decisions about the local provision of services. Phrases that cropped up repeatedly were 'supporting to, not doing for' and 'promoting independence'.

'Our approach has been that housing-related support is about promoting independence, it's about move on, it's about progress.'

'For example, helping to manage a weekly shopping budget could be housing-related support; doing someone's shopping for them every week would be care.'

'Another way of looking at this is to ask "At what point is the only outcome maintenance?" If the only outcome is maintenance, then Supporting People is not appropriate funding because it is designed to promote independence.'

Although these explanations captured the essential distinction between housing-related support and social care, as one housing association officer pointed out, such broad definitions simply meant that the impetus to create a more concrete definition was passed on to provider organisations:

'I don't think there's been any really firm definitions of what housing-related support is from the Supporting People team: they'll come and ask us!'

Deciding eligibility and rationing resources

Despite the lack of clarity from central government, professionals from Supporting People teams, social services, housing departments and health authorities all accepted that, as administrators of a cash-limited budget, they had to decide a set of criteria by which to allocate limited resources fairly.

Our findings from interviews with relevant professionals reveal that, in practice, administering authorities were using six different approaches to determine:

- who was eligible to receive the funding; and
- how the funding could be used.

Each approach resulted in variations in the availability of Supporting People funding and in the scope of the tasks that were permitted.

Excluding those with statutory entitlements

Supporting People officers, in particular, repeatedly highlighted the necessity of limiting funding to those individuals who were in need of support, but whose needs did not constitute a statutory duty of care, as defined under the 1948 National Assistance Act. Where a statutory duty exists, it was argued that support services should be funded from relevant statutory budgets (that is, social services' community care budgets or, where an individual met local criteria for receiving continuing healthcare, NHS budgets).

> 'Our interpretation of the guidance is that if there's a pre-existing need for care services then that supersedes any entitlement to Supporting People. And, of course, we have to remember that there is no statutory entitlement to Supporting People services.'

> 'The financial responsibility for providing services to people who carry a statutory duty should remain with health and social care services.'

People with learning disabilities are more likely to carry a 'statutory duty' than some of the other groups of people who might wish to access Supporting People funds. This means that they have a statutory entitlement (that is, a legal right) to certain support services, funded via either social services or the National Health Service (NHS). It is arguable that anyone with a statutory entitlement to services should access the support they need via this entitlement rather than seek funding from non-statutory budgets. This is because non-statutory budgets such as Supporting People are strictly cash-limited, and accessing these monies, when other sources of funding are available, will deprive someone else – who is not entitled to statutory services – of any service whatsoever.

This was cited as one reason why services for people with learning disabilities were likely to come under particularly close scrutiny when Supporting People budgets came under pressure – because, unlike many other groups of service users, they might be able to access support from other sources. Denying some people with learning disabilities access to Supporting People funding on the grounds that they have a statutory right to services funded by other means does not mean that supported living cannot be an option for these individuals. There is no reason why community care budgets cannot be used to pay for supported living services rather than for more traditional types of support such as residential care.

It was notable that it was Supporting People officers, rather than any other interviewees, who laid an emphasis on determining eligibility in relation to existing statutory duties. The fact that care managers and service commissioners from health and social services departments did not raise the same issue may indicate that they have not engaged with the detail of Supporting People and are perhaps unaware that it is a non-statutory source of funding (or that they do not understand the distinction between statutory and non-statutory services). However, another, arguably more likely, explanation is that care managers and service commissioners are ignoring the wider implications of cost-shunting from a statutory to a non-statutory budget because of the immediate financial pressures under which they operate. These pressures are perhaps so intense that any opportunity to get services funded from a budget other than their own is welcomed.

Adapting government guidelines about eligible tasks

The ODPM issued a non-definitive list of the support tasks that Supporting People monies could be used to pay for. This list, or a local adaptation of this list, was one of the key ways by which administering authorities determined eligibility. However, such an approach proved to be of limited use in restricting the cost of individual packages of support, not least because the lists tended to encompass such a wide variety of support tasks.

One Supporting People officer read out the following list of eligible tasks:

> 'It says: "Help in setting up and maintaining a home or tenancy; developing domestic and life skills; developing social skills; advice, advocacy and liaison; helping managing the finances and any claims; emotional support; counselling and advice; help in gaining access to other services; help in establishing personal safety and security; supervision and monitoring of health and well-being and medication; peer support and befriending; help in finding accommodation; provision of community alarms; help in maintaining safety and security of the home; cleaning of the room; risk assessment; advice and support on repairs and home improvements; handy person services; help with shopping; errands, good neighbour tasks". And so the list goes on: "Access to local community organisations; security; support".'

Another commented:

> 'It's the community living skills, I think, that I would list as housing-related support. It's the personal living skills, like the washing, the personal care and the cooking that I would say are personal care issues.'

Many of the tasks listed left ample scope for varied interpretation; under this approach almost anything other than intimate personal care *could* be classified as housing-related support. Only one case study area used this as their sole means of defining eligibility. It was notable that this administering authority paid for many more high-cost packages of support than authorities that used an 'eligible tasks' list, but in conjunction with other limits on cost, such as those described below.

Limits on the number of hours of support available

Some authorities capped the number of hours of support per week that any one individual could receive. Such limits are set at the discretion of local Supporting People teams and so varied considerably from authority to authority. Among the four administering authorities visited for the purposes of this study, three were introducing limits of this kind. But the limits being introduced varied widely – ranging from 10 hours to 30 hours of support per person per week. All of the following quotes are from Supporting People team members:

> 'We took the line that it should be the greatest good for the greatest number. And, by that, we thought that 10 hours of housing-related support was something we could afford to sustain. Including packages whereby the person was getting the

equivalent of a whole-time support worker in a given week is a patent nonsense. It's not empowering, it's not enabling. And if there's [a need for] that level of support then, as far as we're concerned, it's outside the scope of the Supporting People programme.'

'My view is that you are probably talking about packages, certainly of housing-related support, of no more than two or three hours a day. It's that sort of area. Because if you get over that I think you're into social care. I mean, I can't imagine what housing support would really take more than two hours a day.'

'It's difficult to envisage you would want to give 35 hours per week of that kind of support.... You know, how many times a day would somebody need help to make their building secure, to make shopping lists, to do budgets?'

In practice, however, even where guideline limits on the number of hours of support available per person per week had been introduced, they were often broken because of high support packages inherited as 'legacy funding' from Transitional Housing Benefit (THB). THB is the term used for payments made under the shadow Supporting People programme, which operated for two years before the system went 'live' in April 2003. During this period central government encouraged local providers to access the new funding stream and there were no specified limits to the amount of support that could be provided for an individual service user. As a consequence, many Supporting People teams had inherited some very high-cost individual support packages. There was strong evidence that concerted attempts were being made by Supporting People teams to reduce the size of high-cost packages originating from the era of THB, but it was typically not possible to immediately impose the same restrictions on these existing support packages as it was on new packages of support.

Limits to the maximum number of hours of support available per week were in some senses arbitrary. However, they did help to prevent the 'eligible task' approach from resulting in very high-cost individual packages. It was, perhaps, inevitable that it was Supporting People officers (rather than other interviewees) who showed the greatest attachment to limits on the hours of support available per person per week. Their commitment to this approach appeared to be driven in large part by a utilitarian desire to help as many people as possible – not just those with a learning disability. From this perspective, it is hard to argue that such an approach is unfair.

In practice, however, for people with learning disabilities – particularly those with higher support needs – the approach of limiting the hours per week of available support could preclude them from receiving services funded through Supporting People. However, it could be argued that such individuals could still access other, statutory, funding sources in order to pay for their supported living services.

Limits on the cost per hour of support

Three of our case study areas had either introduced, or were in the process of introducing, limits to the amount per hour that would be paid for the direct support provided to an individual. Again, there were wide discrepancies between areas, with one of the administering authorities we visited setting a limit of £12.05 per hour while another permitted costs to a maximum of £22 per hour. For the most part these differences could be explained by the vagaries of local geography and economies: higher limits were set in more rural areas and in areas with low unemployment, where staff recruitment was more difficult.

The cost per hour of support might also vary between different service user groups, reflecting the different skill levels required of support staff, as explained by more than one Supporting People officer:

'They set a limit on the cost per hour, and I think that's £12.05. And we have a number of services that cost more than that per hour. And the other thing they would look at was the number of hours, per day, each person got. And they set the limit at 14 hours a week, I believe'"

'We could sustain an hourly rate of £22 for specialist services, so people understand the needs of those with learning disability or people with serious mental health issues. Where, you know, there was a staff team that eminently could demonstrate they had the skill base. But really £20 was more in line with what we were looking for.'

From the perspective of Supporting People officers, this approach had a particular advantage: it ensured that an excessive amount of money was not being used by provider organisations for their own administrative purposes. Our analysis of five-year Supporting People strategies, however, suggested that increasing numbers of administering authorities were, in fact, using the cost per hour of support to benchmark their own costs, in relation to regional averages. This appears to have some logic to it, but there is also some risk that it might eventually drive costs down, with services suffering as a result. English regions, or even single administering authorities, can contain wide variations in costs that are fully explicable in terms of local geographic and economic drivers. Pressure to gravitate towards *average* costs will hurt those services that operate in sparsely populated rural areas or in areas with high housing or staffing costs.

Limits on the overall cost of support packages

Evidence from the analysis of five-year Supporting People strategies showed a huge variation in the average costs of Supporting People packages. Differences were apparent both between administering authorities and between different groups of service users in the same administering authority. In most administering authorities, the average cost of support packages for people with learning disabilities was significantly higher than for other groups of service users (see Chapter 4 for further details).

Our interviews shed some light on the way in which the *overall* costs of Supporting People packages were limited. For example, one authority aimed to provide a maximum of 10 hours per person per week of 'floating support' (that is, support from staff who were not based in a particular building but visited individuals in their own flats as required), at a rate of no more than £20 per hour – thus implying that overall costs per week would be no more than £200. By contrast, another authority was happy to pay for packages – wholly funded from Supporting People – that cost more than £500 per person per week (equivalent to over £26,000 per annum). Such huge variation in the cost of individual support packages was not lost on our interviewees:

'I suppose our most expensive would be £510.55 [per week]. But on the other end you've got people on £25.90 a week. And I know the money comes into it, but actually it's the amount of support that people need in order to remain within their own environment.' (Social services manager/commissioner)

'I think the biggest one I've heard of was, what, £4,000 a week for someone.' (Housing association officer)

Importantly, there was explicit recognition, and acceptance, of the fact that support packages for people with learning disabilities might need to be significantly higher than those for some other groups of service users:

> 'Learning disability placements are more expensive. I mean, sheltered accommodation is about, you know, 27 quid a week for the support there in comparison to, normally, around about £250 for the person with a learning disability.' (Supporting People officer)

However, as Supporting People reviews continue across all administering authorities it is likely that pressure to reduce the costs of individual support packages will increase. At the time this research was undertaken, several of the services visited had yet to undergo review; but where reviews had taken place, significant reductions in funding were sometimes being imposed. For example, on the day we visited, one organisation that provided support to four people who shared a tenancy had just been informed that the outcome of the review of their service by the local Supporting People team was that the funded hours of support for the project were to be cut by 35 hours per week, equivalent to losing a full-time member of staff.

Limits on the duration of support

In many of the answers to our questions on eligibility criteria, there was implicit recognition of the fact that people with learning disabilities will often need higher levels of support, over longer periods of time, than other service users. Supporting People guidance from the ODPM differentiates between the provision of short-term and long-term support, the former lasting for no longer than two years. Clearly, the majority of people with learning disabilities are likely to require some level of support for longer than this period.

This was one of the factors that contributed to concern over the costs of individual support packages. Unlike most other groups of service users, such as frail older people, people with mental health difficulties, teenage parents and women fleeing domestic violence, whose need for support is likely to be episodic, or time-limited through changing circumstances or death, people with learning disabilities are likely to require ongoing support throughout their lives:

> 'I don't have a lot of time if people come and say, well, they need 20 hours [of support per week] and they're going to need it forever and a day, because that then isn't enabling housing-related support. I'd argue that that's care.' (Supporting People officer)

In the short term, however, there was often some willingness to be flexible about the implementation of local guidelines, as in the following example from a Supporting People officer in an administering authority where there was normally a maximum of 10 hours of support per week.

> 'If they're taking on a home for the first time, after being in a residential college, they may well need 15, they may well need 20 [hours of support per week] to set them up. I've no problem with that as long as it's continually, consistently and effectively reviewed and that the end game is about maximising that person's independence and it's reduced accordingly.'

Such flexibility may be particularly important for people with learning disabilities who would welcome the opportunity to move out of residential care and into supported living, but who may need a relatively high level of support in the short term while adjusting to their new lifestyle and developing community supports.

On a positive note, there was no evidence, from either the interviews or the analysis of five-year Supporting People strategies, that administering authorities were trying to exclude people with learning disabilities from Supporting People services by limiting the duration of funding. It was recognised that people with learning disabilities were likely to require varying degrees of support throughout their lives, and that the Supporting People review processes could allow support levels to be increased or decreased, in accordance with changes in individual circumstances.

Meeting the higher support needs of people with severe learning disabilities

Opinion was divided among interviewees from different administering authorities and different professional backgrounds as to whether individuals with severe or profound learning disabilities should be accessing Supporting People services:

> 'I think that, you know, learning disability services fit awkwardly into Supporting People in some ways, because the outcomes that we would expect from somebody without a learning disability may not be as achievable for somebody who does have a learning disability.' (Supporting People officer)

> 'I think it probably excludes the people with more profound and severe learning disabilities, who are always going to need help and assistance to actually complete tasks – whereas, I think, the philosophy behind Supporting People is that people are enabled to complete tasks themselves. That's always going to be difficult for those with profound and multiple disabilities. And I think that naturally excludes them from that funding stream.' (Social services manager/commissioner)

As we have seen, it is often not easy to determine the boundary between housing-related support, which *is* eligible for Supporting People funding, and care tasks, which are not. Those people with learning disabilities who have higher support needs may wish to access Supporting People monies to pay for their housing-related support, but also need additional hours of care – funded through local authority community care budgets – in order to be able to maintain an independent lifestyle. Such 'mixed packages' of care, where a seamless service is created by merging funding from more than one agency's budget, are commonplace – but these packages are most often jointly funded by health and social services. Supporting People has the potential to offer an additional source of funding, and this was recognised by interviewees:

> '[People with higher support needs] would go into mixed packages, where part of it will be the Supporting People money and part of it will be social care support.' (Social services manager/commissioner)

Not everybody regarded mixed packages favourably; some thought (as we discussed earlier) that anyone with a statutory entitlement to support should automatically be precluded from Supporting People funding:

> 'To start from the perspective where somebody needs personal care and pay housing-related support, I find difficult to envisage.' (Supporting People officer)

Further debates about the use of mixed packages centred on how the different elements of such a package would be delivered. In contrast to the usual concern of health and social care services to provide a 'seamless' service, Supporting People officers were more likely to argue that, where care was needed in addition to housing support, this should be delivered separately, as in the following examples:

> 'We're very clear about saying "Well, actually these are [housing] support needs and you are a provider that will deal with [housing] support needs. You won't provide for anybody with personal care needs, unless that part of the package is met by an external provider".'

> 'I have problems seeing personal care needs being provided by the same person who's providing your housing-related support. I have problems marrying the two up. They don't make happy bed partners to me.'

In practice some (but by no means all) providers of housing-related support also provided a few hours of care to one or more of their service users. In order to do this, organisations had to be registered as domiciliary care providers. Despite the above quotes, there was some recognition from Supporting People officers that it was best practice for additional care hours to be made available if required because of changing personal circumstances:

> 'I think it's possible to have a package whereby, you know, maybe someone who's suffering from dementia and has a learning disability can be supported by introducing domiciliary care, or a form of personal care.'

In general, Supporting People officers viewed mixed packages of care and support less favourably than their counterparts in health and social services' care management and commissioning teams. It remains to be seen whether Supporting People will increasingly, therefore, become a resource available only to those with lower support needs, or whether – as Supporting People teams gain more confidence in their role – they will become more willing to promote mixed packages of care and support, where appropriate, to meet the needs of some individuals at particular points in their life.

The impact of eligibility criteria on service users: the service provider perspective

Staff in service provider organisations tended to define housing-related support in terms broadly similar to those of staff in administering authorities but their interpretation *and implementation* of eligibility criteria were often subtly at odds with those who held the purse strings.

None of the people interviewed from support provider organisations described or defined housing-related support in a way that was incompatible with the approach taken by their local Supporting People team. However, alongside this shared understanding, a strong sense of frustration also emerged with the lack of absolute clarity on the definition. There were two particular reasons for their discomfort. The first, and most important, was the impact that changes or restrictions to eligibility had on service users directly. The second was the negative impact they feared any such changes would have on the finances of their own (provider) organisations – and again, indirectly, on service users.

Loss of support to engage in social activities

A number of service providers had been given no choice but to be transferred from operating under social services' community care budgets to Supporting People funding. Notably, these interviewees did not mention (or appear aware) that this marked a shift from a statutory to a non-statutory funding stream. However, they were acutely aware of the effect that the change of funding had had on their ability to support services users as they saw best. This was not about money in itself, since the overall amount of financial support provided had not necessarily changed, but rather was about the restrictions that Supporting People imposed on the *type* of support that services were allowed to provide. In some cases, they reported that service users had found the changes to their support difficult to adjust to:

> 'I think it was pretty unfair on quite a lot of the service users, at the time, and quite unfair on our staff team, because they were getting quite ... people were getting quite anxious and sometimes quite angry about the change and wanted to go back to social services, obviously, to be supported and have a much more broader remit.' (Manager of supported living service)

The tasks that were most frequently referred to as being no longer eligible for support, but which service users had valued greatly, were support to engage in social activities and support to find or maintain employment. Support providers were often convinced of the importance of these 'non-eligible' tasks in the life of their service users. They had therefore found a number of ways of bending the rules, sometimes (literally) at their own expense, in order to continue this kind of provision, as shown in the following exchange:

> 'We'd also got hours down for social, which they weren't really happy about. But my argument was that these three people ... it was the most important aspect of their lives (was their social lives) and because of their disabilities they needed staff to actually take them and do things with them as they haven't got the ability to do it themselves.'

> *Interviewer:* 'And did they go for that? Did the Supporting People team go for that?'

> 'Not really, no, because it wasn't under the criteria. But saying that, we've used, probably, the hours which are allocated for other things, to do those things. And we, obviously, do a lot more hours than we get paid for.'

Loss of support to maintain employment

The manager of another service was also exasperated with what she saw as the short-sightedness of precluding certain activities from the list of eligible tasks, although in this instance the particular focus was on support for employment:

> 'Now, whether they were on the original lists and they are no longer there.... Things like supporting somebody in a workplace. So, for example, we support people who want a job, who either want support going to a job centre, finding a DEA [Disability Employment Adviser], understanding about tax credits. We support several people who struggle in their job and, every now and then, the manager gets a call saying "We're about to sack, Fred". Or "He's on a last written warning. Can we have a meeting with you?" So we do things like that.... Either we've got to undersell ourselves in the future, and say we don't do these things very much – which isn't really true, we do do those things. Or we stick our neck on the block and say, "Actually, it's a holistic service, we do whatever that person needs and is asking us to do".'

Adjusting to sudden reductions in funding

Support providers who were experiencing reductions in funding as a result of the Supporting People review process were also, not surprisingly, critical of the impact this was having on service users. Importantly, however, their dissatisfaction was more to do with the rapidity of the reduction funding, rather than with the principle that Supporting People should only pay for a limited number of hours of support per person.

> 'Some of the people we started working with started with 30, 40 hours a week. So to suddenly say "Right, you're down to 10 hours" has been very difficult for people. But the new people that we're starting work with were told, quite clearly, 10 hours is a maximum, unless we're supporting somebody to move from residential care into their own home and then, for a period of possibly six weeks, while they get settled in and things are set up they can have up to 15. But that's it.'

Providers understood that this was a problem that had not been created by their local Supporting People team. More often it had come about as a result of social services' previous encouragement to providers to make claims for THB, which subsequently proved to be unsustainable under the Supporting People programme. Several managers of support provider organisations spoke openly about the distortions that had been introduced into the Supporting People system as a consequence of THB:

> 'When they came over the hours that they were allocated was quite considerable. And, in many cases, it was over and above the needs of the individual.'

> 'I think they [social services] weren't aware of where the money was coming from. Because it wasn't new money, it was old money that was floating all about. And, OK, they see that [THB] as being funded from central government, not from the local boroughs, so they wanted that money so they were quite pushy in saying "This is support".'

The belief that, at least in some areas, or to a certain degree, social services departments had sought to use THB and Supporting People as a means of cost-shunting support for people with learning disabilities out of their community care budgets, was a common one, which we discussed in the Introduction. There was considerable concern among support providers that, as a result of this, service users were being made vulnerable through inadequate levels of support or that gaps in support were emerging that would be detrimental to their overall well-being.

In this context, the limited availability of jointly funded packages of support was acutely felt. Support providers in some areas were getting a minimal number of hours of care, funded from social services budgets, in addition to Supporting People funding. More often, however, social services were depicted as unwilling to pick up the tab for activities that lay beyond the remit of Supporting People. Those who worked in support provider organisations frequently complained about the difficulties they experienced in trying to patch together different sources of funding into a holistic package:

> 'Some people have a joint package. But the package of domiciliary care is very low. I mean, we're not talking about packages of, you know, 100 hours of care and 10 hours of support. We're talking about maybe 10 hours of support and two hours of care for specific pieces of domiciliary care, specific pieces of work that people will do alongside their housing-related support.'

'We haven't even bothered applying for extra hours [of care, funded by social services] because they just won't let us have those extra hours. There's just no point.'

'Social services, in all local authorities, insisted we moved across to Supporting People anyway. It's extremely unlikely that most of those social services would pick up the tab for the bit left over.'

'For people in our supported living home, when we try and get social care support for them our learning disability team say, "They're not our responsibility 'cos they're not in registered care homes". Whereas Supporting People are saying, "It's not housing-related support".'

Harsh choices for providers

At the heart of the difficulties that support provider organisations faced in trying to operate within the boundaries of Supporting People definitions of housing-related support and associated eligibility criteria was their desire to provide holistic services, which promoted the rights and independence of service users. Whenever the fulfilment of this ambition lay beyond the remit of Supporting People, provider organisations were faced with the harsh choice of providing support for which they were not being paid – thus threatening their own financial stability – or with providing services that they feared were not adequately meeting the needs of their service users.

A number of support providers were coming round to the idea that Supporting People funding should, therefore, be more explicitly targeted on people with lower support needs. However, any move to put this into operation was recognised as presenting a significant challenge, not least regarding the fate of people with higher support needs who were currently receiving support funded from Supporting People:

'I think some people have been wrongly placed and then they're going to have to find them alternative placements. And that's going to be difficult because their residential places are closing and they don't have anywhere to put them.'

'We've all come into Supporting People with our own ideas and because nothing's been written down and there's no clear boundaries around if you need 10 hours of care a week you can be in Supporting People, but if you need 35 hours of care you need to be in residential care. Each case is taken on its own merit, which it should be, but it depends who decides on that case.'

Encouraging good practice

We conclude this chapter with a 'good practice' checklist. This is not intended to be prescriptive but to encourage those who work with Supporting People funding to think systematically about the different outcomes for people with learning disabilities associated with various ways of delivering housing and support, based on the evidence of this study.

Good practice checklist 1: Setting local eligibility criteria

(1) What elements are you using to determine the eligibility of services for Supporting People funding?
  (a) Eligible and non-eligible tasks
  (b) Limit on number of hours of support per week
  (c) Limit on cost of support per hour
  (d) Limit on cost of support per week
  (e) Limit on overall cost of support
  (f) Limit on duration of support

(2) How transparent are your eligibility criteria?
  (a) Do provider organisations understand them?
  (b) Do tenants and support workers understand them?
  (c) Are they reviewed regularly?

(3) How do your existing eligibility criteria impact on existing and potential service users?
  (a) Are certain groups excluded from services?
  (b) Is extra support available, at least in the short term, to people moving into independent living for the first time?
  (c) Can levels of support be varied as individual support needs change over the lifecourse or in response to changes in personal circumstances?

(4) Do you encourage or discourage the use of 'mixed packages' of support and care?
  (a) Why?
  (b) What impact does this have on service users?
  (c) Which service users might benefit from mixed packages?

(5) Do you routinely check whether individuals carry a 'statutory duty' and are therefore entitled to receive funding from other sources?

2

Dimensions of difference in housing and support

This chapter reports on the location and range of housing that people with learning disabilities in the study were living in and the extent to which the tenancy rights and responsibilities that should accompany Supporting People were recognised (or not) by our interviewees. It also explores two key dimensions of difference in the structuring of Supporting People services in the areas studied. These were first, whether people lived alone (individual tenancies) or with others (shared tenancies) and second, whether they received floating support (staff visiting their homes to help with specific tasks) or accommodation-based support (staff based in tenants' homes and working shifts there).

Housing

In theory, Supporting People offers people with learning disabilities the same range of housing options as other independent adults, including home ownership and renting in the private sector as well as renting from a local authority or registered social landlord (housing association). In practice, the choices for people with learning disabilities in the study were limited by their lack of income – most of the tenants we spoke to were living on benefits and the few who did have jobs were in voluntary or low-paid work. Although owner-occupation is slowly becoming a possibility for some people with learning disabilities, we did not meet any learning disabled owner-occupiers who received Supporting People monies for their housing-related support. Supporting People teams, however, were keen to stress that this was not because they were unwilling to consider such a possibility. One Supporting People team was already actively involved in enabling home ownership for people with learning disabilities:

> 'The other thing I would like you to be aware of is we're very proactively involved in promoting shared ownership through the SOLD [Shared Ownership for People with Learning Disabilities] programme. Last year, we used up the entire allocation of ... probably six or seven shared ownerships went through, which may not sound a lot in the overall scheme of things but....'[1]

Rented accommodation and tenancies

All of the tenants whom we interviewed for this project, then, lived in rented accommodation. Despite this common factor, there was huge diversity in relation to all other respects of people's housing. Most tenants were in property belonging to registered social landlords (housing associations). A significant minority lived in homes owned by local authority housing departments and a small number lived in property that was either

---

[1] See References for further details on SOLD.

privately owned or owned by a charitable trust. There were no observable differences in tenants' lifestyles that could be attributed to their landlord type.

All recipients of Supporting People monies have a legally binding tenancy agreement with their landlord, unlike the many thousands of people with learning disabilities who live in registered residential care homes or accommodation provided directly by the NHS. Tenancy agreements create both individual rights and responsibilities. Most important for people with learning disabilities is the right that a tenancy gives to remain living in a particular property for the duration of the tenancy agreement, so long as rent is paid and other terms and conditions (for example, not causing a nuisance to neighbours) are met. This is in sharp contrast to the experiences of people with learning disabilities living *without* legal tenancies, who may legally be moved out of their home and into alternative accommodation at the behest of their service provider.

Awareness of tenancy rights and responsibilities

We asked all interviewees, including tenants, support staff, managers of provider organisations, Supporting People teams, social services, housing and other officials, about their understanding of tenancy agreements. Very few interviewees had a full understanding of just how important a tenancy agreement was, and the extent to which it conferred rights and power to people with learning disabilities.

Of the 31 tenants with learning disabilities to whom we spoke, only a small minority (three) knew that they had a tenancy agreement and understood at some level what this meant. Most interviewees did not know whether they had a tenancy agreement because they did not know what a tenancy agreement was. This was the case even when housing associations had invested considerable time and effort in producing tenancy agreements in easy language and/or pictorial versions.

The few tenants who did have some understanding of their tenancy agreement described it in terms of 'knowing their rights' and 'knowing what I have to agree to'. However, there was considerably more evidence of the latter than the former: most interviewees understood that there were certain rules, or conditions, that they had to meet in order to continue living in their home. A typical comment from a tenant was a statement of their responsibilities, such as:

  'We have rules. We have to keep the house clean and tidy and do the washing.'

By contrast, no tenant was able to explain what their *rights* as a tenant were, despite occasionally mentioning them. They appeared unaware that – in theory – they had the right to decide who came into their home to provide the support they needed, or that such support was no longer intrinsically connected to the physical provision of their home. The lack of knowledge around the legal rights inherent in their tenancy undoubtedly impeded the ability of tenants to assert such rights, a situation that is examined in detail in Chapter 3.

Support staff, who had day-to-day contact with tenants and were directly responsible for supporting tenants to assert their rights, were equally ignorant about the rights associated with tenancies. Support staff often emphasised the 'responsibilities' side of holding a tenancy, while overlooking the 'rights'. The following comments from support staff were fairly typical:

'You try and explain to them what this tenancy agreement is and they'll just nod at you. I don't think they have a great understanding of what it actually means. But we do try and say, "Well, look, if you don't pay your rent, you know, you may lose your property".'

'They are all aware that they're responsible for the upkeep and the cleaning and the way their flats are kept. They are all very aware of that.'

One support worker even gave an example of a manager having words with a tenant because "he is not letting us support with cleaning his room". None of these interviewees explicitly linked tenancies to individuals' rights in any way.

It would be wrong to infer from these findings that support staff were knowingly undermining the rights of tenants. Support staff, were, in fact, very keen to promote tenants' rights, as will be seen in the next chapter. But they often had very limited legal knowledge and sometimes lacked an understanding that 'rights' referred to more than being able to choose what to eat for tea, or whether to go to cookery classes.

Local authority housing officers and housing association officers were, by contrast, acutely aware of both the legal significance of tenancy agreements and the ignorance of colleagues in many support provider organisations about them. Unlike others who we interviewed, housing professionals were keen to emphasise the rights accorded to individuals via tenancy agreements, and to stress that such rights applied equally to *all* tenants. However, they remained concerned that provider organisations had not taken on board the impact that tenancies could have on their operations. In particular, they believed that providers were unaware that they would no longer be automatically able to move on 'difficult' tenants. As one housing association officer explained:

'If someone with a learning disability is presenting with some form of difficult, challenging behaviour, often the first response from the support provider is "They'll have to move". Now, they can't just move, they've got an issue with tenancy 'cos we offer the most secure form of tenure and so they've got an assured tenancy agreement. I don't think support providers fully understand what that means and the rights that it gives to people.'

This concern was not altogether unfounded, but was sometimes perhaps misplaced. Providers of housing-related support services interviewed for this study (by which we mean senior staff within support provider organisations; people not involved in giving day-to-day support to tenants) were all aware that the people they supported did have tenancy agreements and they regarded their key role as a support service to be, in the words of one interviewee, "supporting our service users to maintain their tenancy". Some even spoke explicitly about both responsibilities *and* rights:

'Having tenancy rights and the rights of tenancies has, obviously, got to give them security now, yes. But it's also the responsibilities of being a tenant, as well.'

Interviewer: 'And do you think most tenants are aware of both the rights and the responsibilities that that brings with it?'

'Our tenants…. Our tenants are. They tell us about them quite regularly. "You can't do that, I'm a tenant in this house".

Of course, it may be that not *all* service provider organisations are so well informed, or so supportive of tenants' rights. Indeed, some interviewees from social services departments gave examples of service providers trying to move people out of their homes because of 'unacceptable behaviour', while a service provider in turn criticised a social worker who had likewise attempted to move a tenant out of his home:

> 'We did have an incident, a couple of weeks ago, where there was an incident in one of our supported living houses. And his social worker phoned me up and said, "We're moving him to respite, today". And I said to them, "Is he agreeing to that?" And they're like, "What?" I'm like, "Well, if he's not, you can't move him from his house, as a tenant. If you want us to go through an eviction process with him...." But they were actually just going to say, "Well, we're going to move him 'cos he's not suitable for there anymore". "No, you can't".'

Perhaps it is inevitable that interviewees will point the finger at organisations other than their own. However, the very fact that such examples of poor practice were so easy to come by suggests that a significant amount of work remains to be done to ensure that all staff working with people with learning disabilities fully understand what a tenancy means.

In theory, supported living should mean the separation of the provision of physical housing from the provision of support. But according to both housing officers and Supporting People team members we spoke to, this separation had not always occurred. In a number of the schemes we visited, either a specialist housing association or a local authority acted as *both* landlord *and* provider of housing-related support. This situation has the potential to undermine the impact of rights gained through tenancy, by handing too much power to a single organisation. An awareness of this problem had led several Supporting People teams to express a preference for funding 'floating' (that is, visiting) support. (Floating support is more fully described later in the chapter.) They regarded this as a way of actively promoting a future where there would be less emphasis on specialist housing for people with learning disabilities and more take-up of independent individual tenancies with the local authority, a registered social landlord or within the private rented sector. Some also expressed the hope that the centrality of tenancy to Supporting People would enable people with learning disabilities, and others, to get better access to mainstream housing: the fact of recognising an individual as capable of holding a tenancy was, for some local authority housing departments, the first step to getting onto their housing waiting list.

The quality of housing

The quality of the 'bricks and mortar' aspect of people's homes was generally satisfactory, with no obvious structural or maintenance problems visible to the researchers (such as leaking roofs or extreme damp). All of the rural homes we visited were of a very high standard in terms of their physical construction. The same could not always be said of all the homes in cities or towns. Some of these homes – particularly those owned by a local authority – were of less good quality and/or were situated in run-down areas. In general, homes owned by housing associations appeared typically to be of higher quality. Of course, this could simply reflect the different stock-holdings of the different housing providers.

Location and types of housing

There was considerable variation in the location and types of people's homes visited in our study, which we have broadly categorised as urban housing, rural housing and clustered tenancies.

Urban housing

A wider range of housing options was available in urban areas than in more rural areas; this is probably a reflection of the wider availability of housing stock in urban areas. The range of accommodation we encountered spanned the following:

- shared houses – often, but not always, located in 'good' neighbourhoods. These included:
  - residential care homes that had been deregistered and were now designated as supported living services;
  - ordinary houses on ordinary streets that had been purchased by housing associations with the specific intention of providing supported living;
- individual flats – these varied hugely in type, location and clustering. Examples we came across included:
  - a high-rise inner-city tower block, owned by the local authority, with learning disabled tenants clustered on two floors;
  - individual flats, owned by housing associations, scattered across a local authority area;
  - individual flats, owned by the local authority, all within easy walking distance of one another (a KeyRing scheme, whereby tenants are actively supported to support one another and to develop natural networks of social support from within the local community);
  - an ex-local authority home for older people, now converted internally into individual flats, but still having a shared entrance hall;
  - individual flats, built on the upper floors of a group home for people with learning disabilities, with a shared entrance hall.

All of the urban supported living schemes had certain advantages over those in the countryside, being close to local shops and other amenities and with easy access to public transport. Some flats and shared houses were in well-to-do neighbourhoods. However, it is perhaps inevitable, under a market-driven economic system, that people with learning disabilities – who typically rely on benefits or low-paid jobs for their income – will not tend to have access to the best-quality housing. We found several examples of supported living services based in local authority properties that were far from ideal, including flats over two floors of a tower block on a run-down estate and flats in a converted old people's home, which had been built in the 1960s from glass and concrete and from the outside resembled a low-rise office block or school rather than homes.

Interestingly, however, the managers and staff in both of the above schemes strongly believed that they were offering 'an excellent model for supported living'. In their eyes, any deficit in terms of bricks and mortar was compensated for by the way in which the clustering of individual tenancies made more consistent support possible. The benefits of such clustered tenancies were perceived to include both increased personal safety and social activities:

'Say there's 10 flats, if they're all dotted round everywhere it's very difficult to do a groupy thing or, you know, have a bingo night or.... Whereas, the.... It's a really good model and I feel that is the best model for supported living, in my eyes. And a lot of people might say, oh, it's a bit institutionalised in that way. But it's not because, you know, they don't get support 24 hours – but there's somebody on duty for somebody else, on the hours, and the risk is less and they're not isolated. So, to me, it's the best model I know.' (Support worker)

When visiting these schemes it was impossible *not* to conclude that here were examples of vulnerable people being housed in accommodation that nobody else wanted or would accept. Flats in the tower block had been made available for supported living precisely *because* they were hard to let; the small estate on which they were located was very run down and had problems with antisocial behaviour, including drugs and prostitution. The converted old people's home still retained an institutional air and could not realistically be described as 'ordinary' housing.

However, the value to tenants of clustering individual tenancies (as described later in the chapter) should not be underestimated, despite the less than ideal physical surroundings of these two particular schemes. Not all clustered tenancies were in poor-quality housing or undesirable neighbourhoods. And this type of arrangement typically enabled tenants to benefit from the friendship and safety of having one another as neighbours, while retaining the privacy and independence of their own individual flat.

Rural housing

As we have already indicated, the types of housing available to people with learning disabilities were more limited in range. In our study we found the following:

- shared houses:
  - an intentional community where people with learning disabilities lived alongside non-disabled people and farmed together;
  - a converted barn on a smallholding providing accommodation for three men who received support through an independent organisation run by the farmer and his wife. (All three tenants of this property had previously lived in a residential care home run by the same couple in a town.)
- newly built low-rise flats, owned by a housing association, in the centre of a small market town.

Rural life may not suit everyone, but the people we met appeared to have chosen actively to swap the convenience of town or city (in terms of easy access to public transport and amenities) for the more immediate freedoms of the countryside. In all of the rural settings we visited, people with significant degrees of learning disability were afforded a high degree of independence – made possible in part because the location of their home protected them from the dangers posed by traffic and crime.

Support

The purpose of Supporting People is to enable people to attain, or maintain, independent tenancies. As we established in Chapter 1, the funded support is focused very clearly on *housing-related support*, rather than offering support for other areas of tenants' lives – such as personal care or social and educational activities. Unless additional funds are available – for example from local authority community care budgets or from the nationally administered Independent Living Fund – the restriction of support to housing-related tasks undoubtedly limits the ability of some people with learning disabilities to access supported living. However, for people in the study who were receiving supported living services, the factor that appeared to have the biggest impact on their lives was whether they received 'accommodation-based' or 'floating' support.

Accommodation-based support

Accommodation-based support is support provided by a team of staff working in a single location. This was the model of support usually offered to people whose supported living scheme comprised a shared tenancy in a large house. Under the rubric of Supporting People, the needs of each tenant would be assessed individually and a set number of hours of support officially allocated to each person. In practice, the end result was typically the employment of a team of staff, based in the house, who were on hand 24 hours a day, working shifts on a rota basis.

Support staff in these houses were keen to describe how the support they offered differed radically from that provided in residential care homes. They emphasised the focus on individual, rather than group, activities and the way in which routine was brushed aside in favour of enabling each tenant to choose how they wished to live. The role of support staff was described as 'supporting people to learn, rather than providing care'. This was in comparison to residential care, which one interviewee characterised as "actually quite horrific" – places where, in her view, residents had no choices, were not allowed to cook, were not given any money, and had "everything done for them".

In truth, however, there was often little to distinguish some of these establishments from well-run, person-centred, registered care homes. Staff in shared tenancies with accommodation-based support usually had use of one room in the house as an office. Although it was usually emphasised that tenants were welcome in offices, this was sometimes a rather limited welcome:

> 'There's no, like, areas in the house where they're not allowed to go. But obviously, in the office, because of all the things that are in there, it's only when there's a member of staff in there.... Other times it's locked so no one could actually go in, unless there was a member of staff.' (Support worker)

For many proponents of supported living, the existence of staff offices in tenants' homes raises fundamental questions about people's access and control over their own living space. In fact, for some, the existence of a staff office would preclude a building from being truly regarded as a supported living establishment. Indeed, the Association for Supported Living (ASL, 2004) unequivocally states that "There should not be an office for use by support staff in the property".

The supported living services that felt most like residential care homes were, perhaps inevitably, those that were, indeed, deregistered care homes. Despite the best attempts of staff and managers to move towards more individualised support and a greater focus on promoting independence, the required change in underlying ethos could be slow to emerge.

Such difficulties were *not* in evidence to the same degree, however, in shared tenancies with accommodation-based support, which had been designed from the outset as supported living services.

There were, moreover, some clear advantages associated with accommodation-based support. In particular, the fact that at least one member of staff was on duty at any given time maximised the flexibility of support available to tenants. It was, for example, possible for tenants in some of these services to change their plans at the last minute, because someone was always on hand to provide whatever support might be needed for any given activity.

Floating support

Floating support means staff who visit tenants in their homes in order to provide support for specific tasks, but who have an office base elsewhere. In contrast to accommodation-based support, floating support was typically used to provide support to people who had individual tenancies (or, less commonly, to couples who lived together).

In many senses, floating support created services that were truer to the philosophy of supported living. Tenants were always clearly in charge of their own homes and support was always given on a one-to-one basis. In this framework there was no danger that the roles of support provider would become confused with that of landlord. The idea of a tenant choosing to change their support provider organisation was, therefore, a *real* possibility, rather than merely a theoretical one.

There were, however, some difficulties and disadvantages:

- *Meeting peaks and troughs in demand:* Support hours were not pooled, as they typically were in a shared tenancy, so individual tenants could only receive a limited number of hours of staff contact per day. This was fine for tenants who had employment or other regular activities and a strong network of family and friends, but sometimes left other people feeling isolated and lonely. Furthermore, despite the best efforts of support provider organisations, it was not always possible for every person to receive their support at the times they wished. Inevitably, when providers were responsible for delivering support to a number of tenants each of whom lived alone, demand for support peaked at certain times of day. For example, many tenants needed support to prepare an evening meal, so demand for support was high between 5pm and 7pm.

- *Inflexible hours:* The fact that staff were not on hand 24 hours a day meant that it was not easy to change support hours at short notice. Support provider organisations did their best to be as flexible as possible, and all offered an out-of-hours on-call service for emergencies, but most required at least 24 hours notice in order to change staff hours. For the more able and independent tenants who did not require daily support this was less of a problem, but it did limit the ability of many less able tenants to act spontaneously. One partial solution that at least one support provider organisation had adopted was to employ part-time rather than full-time staff, as this maximised the flexibility of staff rotas.

Table 1 (overleaf) presents the advantages and disadvantages of different ways of providing accommodation and support.

Combining the approaches in 'clustered' individual tenancies

One of the advantages of individual tenancies being clustered in a particular locale, or even being in a single block, was that it offered the potential for having the best of both worlds – the independence and privacy of individual tenancies, coupled with the flexibility of support and social aspects of group living. In practice we found that this positive combination was only occasionally achieved, because it relied on flexible and imaginative staffing. The clustered individual tenancies that we visited as part of this study demonstrated both ends of the spectrum.

In one clustered scheme the support provider employed part-time staff, usually with no background in care work, and gave them comprehensive values-based training at the start of their employment. The result was that tenants received high-quality individualised support from staff, and further support from one another. This enabled people with a significant degree of learning disability to take real control of their own lives and maintain their own home and tenancy.

Table 1: The advantages and disadvantages associated with different ways of providing accommodation and support

Shared tenancies and accommodation–based support	Individual tenancies and floating support
Danger of less individualised support	Fully individual support
24–hour staff cover sometimes possible	Limited number of support hours available each day
Maximum flexibility of support	Difficult to change support hours at short notice
Less privacy/time alone	More privacy/time alone
Less chance of being lonely	More chance of being lonely
Support and housing often managed by the same organisation	Clear separation between landlord and support provider
Possibility of minimising costs per hour of support	Potentially higher costs per hour of support, because of the need to allow for staff travel time
System suited to the employment of full–time support staff – giving greater consistency of support	System suited to the employment of part–time staff – giving greater flexibility of support

By contrast, another clustered scheme employed full-time staff, many if not most of whom had backgrounds in residential care. Staff here worked traditional shift patterns that did not allow for additional support to be available at 'peak' times. As a consequence, the individual support that each tenant required in order to prepare an evening meal was provided on a rota basis. This allocated 30 minutes to each person, starting at 4pm, which was clearly less than satisfactory.

Social activities and community integration

It was beyond the scope of our study to explore in detail the daily lives of all the people with learning disabilities with whom we spoke. Other studies, however, have demonstrated the extent to which the lives of many people with learning disabilities are impoverished by poor-quality day services, limited access to education and a lack of employment opportunities (Beyer et al, 2004; DWP, 2006). Many of the tenants we interviewed were, in stark contrast to this picture, engaged in a broad range of daily activities, including paid employment and voluntary work; social firms (not-for-profit organisations whose purpose is to provide employment and contribute meaningfully to the local community); adult education classes; traditional day centres; and sport. However, the availability of support to enable individuals to undertake any of these activities depended on the eligibility criteria set by local Supporting People teams, as we reported in Chapter 1. This was, in effect, a postcode lottery: with attitudes among Supporting People officers towards funding such activities ranging from listing 'access to community organisations' as one of their eligible housing-related support tasks, through to bluntly declaring that "Whilst it may well be desirable and it may improve quality of life to go out and support them [tenants with learning disabilities] to access activities in the local community, that is not the role of the Supporting People programme".

Supporting people to be active in their community

The extent to which tenants *were* able to develop fuller lives, in which they were supported to be active members of their local community, depended on the presence of one or more of the following factors:

- a local definition of housing-related support that did not preclude support for social or employment-related activities;
- being able to get to and from activities independently – which might involve crossing roads, using public transport and/or having the money to pay for a taxi;
- living in a shared tenancy, with 24-hour accommodation-based support;
- having a network of friends and family living nearby who were willing and able to offer support;
- living in a pleasant neighbourhood, where it was safe to go out alone – even at night.

In more than one area where supported living services had existed prior to Supporting People, but were now financed through this programme rather than through community care budgets, there was a belief that the rigidity of Supporting People eligibility criteria had *reduced* the availability of support for social and community activities. This was especially so in relation to evening activities, which were typically regarded by Supporting People teams as being 'simply social', rather than as a vital, integral part of being a fully participating member of the local community.

In considering social support, however, it should be borne in mind that social service commissioners do not operate under the same restrictive criteria as those of Supporting People teams. There is therefore nothing to prevent extra hours of 'social' support being funded from community care budgets in order to ensure that tenants receive an appropriate balance of support overall. The fact that this seldom appeared to happen is indicative of a failure of services to collaborate effectively. The causes of this may be linked to the extent to which some social services commissioners have regarded Supporting People as an opportunity to cost-shunt, or may be linked to the fact that some Supporting People teams are working with people with mild learning disabilities who would typically not meet the criteria for social service intervention. Whatever the reasons behind it, the failure to fund social support is a problem that adversely affected the lives of a significant proportion of tenants with learning disabilities.

Becoming part of a community

As with other 'community-based' service developments for people with learning disabilities, supported living – or at least the type of supported living that Supporting People teams are able to fund – can be criticised for promoting *community presence* but doing little to encourage, or enable, social or *community integration*.

Assessing the extent to which individuals are meaningfully engaged with their local community is not an easy task, and arguably a highly subjective one. For this study we took the view that community engagement should mean that tenants had some kind of social or emotional support network that extended beyond paid staff. It was clear that, judged on this basis, few tenants were actively involved in their local communities.

The people who were most likely to have strong community support networks were:

- those who had moved into a supported tenancy directly from their family home rather than having previously lived in an institutional setting;
- people whose families lived nearby and visited regularly;
- younger people.

Those who did not have such strong support networks to rely on were in danger of being lonely, particularly if they lived alone. One tenant who admitted to sometimes feeling lonely described his life in the following terms: "I just sit around all the time and get bored. I can't go out on my own. I go out with staff. I wish they could get more staff so that I could go out more". Others complained that they had "too much time by myself".

The understanding that high-quality supported living services should do more than offer a roof and food was only catching on slowly, but at least one Supporting People officer had the measure of this problem:

> 'I think the threat of social isolation is also a big one that we have to be very careful not to miss. So it's hard to plan services for people with learning disabilities because, I suspect, that although people are asking for independent single tenancies, they actually need to be near somebody who is going to provide them with some emotional and friendship support because that's often what's missing from their lives. And that's not to do, necessarily, with their ability to function.'

Few of the support staff we interviewed believed that it was, or even could be, part of their role to support and enable the development of tenants' natural support networks within the local community. The same was true of most other groups of professionals, with the notable exception of social services personnel. Perhaps because of the particular emphasis placed on issues of power, discrimination and social stratification within social work education, these interviewees were more likely to refer to the failure of Supporting People services to support social integration:

> *Interviewer:* 'What benefits do you think accrue to tenants from being in supported living?'

> 'Umm.... I'd like to say ... I'd like to say being part of community. Umm, I'm not sure a great amount of that's happening at the moment.' (Social services manager)

In some cases, social workers linked people's social isolation to the fact that supported living schemes did not "tend to be in the most affluent areas". Several also gave examples of how involvement in local networks was "not necessarily in the service users' 'best interest'" and had given rise to adult protection issues, an issue that will be discussed in more depth in Chapter 3.

Finally, it is worth highlighting the fact that tenants were for the most part unaware of the bureaucratic restraints placed on support workers as to which tasks they could and could not perform. In many instances, support staff were the tenants' most regular visitors and provided the bulk of their interaction with other people. When asked to describe what made a good support worker, tenants used terms such as 'nice', 'kind', 'helpful' and 'a friend'. In other words, from the perspective of tenants, support staff fulfilled a role that was as much about social and emotional support, as it was about the specific housing-related task (such as assistance to prepare a meal, or support to pay household bills) that they were 'officially' undertaking. This begs the question whether staff, whose remit did not formally extend to social and emotional support, were placed in an untenable position.

Encouraging good practice

We have grouped our findings relating to positive practice in housing and support into three areas: tenancy rights and responsibilities; accessing housing; and providing the right support, each with its own Good Practice Checklist.

Tenancy rights and responsibilities

All parties involved in the provision of both housing and support need to fully understand the rights and responsibilities associated with tenancies. In particular, support staff need to be able to offer accurate information to tenants, such that a tenancy becomes a way of promoting individual rights (for example to get repairs undertaken in good time) rather than predominantly a means of imposing restrictive standards of behaviour (for example tidiness) on individuals.

Good practice checklist 2: Rights, responsibilities and tenancies

- What types of tenancies (see Glossary) are issued to tenants with learning disabilities by your agency? Is a simplified/jargon-free version of the tenancy agreement available to tenants? Has someone gone through it with them?
- Does the simplified tenancy agreement explain the *rights* as well as the *responsibilities* that the agreement confers?
- Have support staff been given training on tenancy agreements and the implications these may have for the way in which they offer support and advice to tenants?
- Have the circumstances in which a tenancy might be terminated been made clear to all parties?
- Where people live in shared accommodation, what contingencies are in place to arbitrate if a serious disagreement arises *between* tenants?

Location and access to housing

The location of people's housing (in a rural or urban area; in a pleasant, safe neighbourhood or otherwise; with easy access, or not, to public transport and local amenities) affected the quality of life of tenants in our study. But this was tempered, or exacerbated, by other factors, including whether accommodation was in individual or shared properties; the availability and flexibility of support; and the extent to which individuals had managed to develop or maintain family, friendship or other social ties within their local community.

Good practice checklist 3: Accessing housing

- Are people with learning disabilities supported to get their names on housing waiting lists of local councils and/or housing associations?
- Where choice-based lettings systems are in operation, are people with learning disabilities supported to take part?
- Where there are long waiting lists for social housing, are people with learning disabilities being supported to investigate the option of renting in the private sector?
- Is the option of home ownership being made available to people with learning disabilities supported in your area or agency?
- What frameworks for housing and support are available in your area or agency?
  - Individual tenancies?
  - Clustered tenancies?
  - Shared tenancies?
- Are individuals given an informed choice between these options?
- Are the likely advantages and disadvantages of each option explained to them, in a way that they can understand?

Enabling staff to provide the right support

It was clear that the 'most skilled' staff were able to support even people with high levels of need to live lives that balanced independence with making and maintaining links with family, friends and local community. Staff who were less skilled tended to focus more on the practical, rather than the emotional or relational, aspects of tenants' welfare. As a consequence, these tenants tended to be more dependent on staff and less well integrated into their local community.

In all services the ability of staff to respond flexibly to the needs of individual tenants was limited by a variety of factors. In general terms, there appeared to be a trade-off of benefits between different kinds of tenancies. Individual tenancies tended to offer greater independence but less flexible support, while shared tenancies had the potential (because of the greater availability of staff) to offer more flexible support, but afford people less independence.

Good practice checklist 4: Providing the right support

- Is there a clear separation between housing and support in local provision, so that organisations do not act as both landlord and support provider to any individual?
- How are tenants supported to become more socially integrated in their local community? If local Supporting People interpretation precludes this, what additional funding could be drawn in?
- What training might staff need to maximise their ability to support tenants' social activities and involvement in local networks and activities?

Choice, control and independence

Promoting choice and independence is at the heart of the Supporting People programme and is also central to the *Valuing People* White Paper (DH, 2001). This chapter explores the extent to which tenants in this study were (or were not) in control of making choices about how to live their lives, and how they were (or were not) supported to attain or maintain maximum independence. It highlights positive changes that have occurred as a result of the Supporting People programme and identifies areas where choice and independence may still be lacking in tenants' lives.

It also explores the relationship between choice, independence and 'risk' and questions the desirability or otherwise of regulatory control of services for people with learning disabilities. It concludes with a review of the extent to which people with learning disabilities were involved in the consultation process leading to the production of administering authorities' five-year strategic plans.

What do choice, control and independence mean in practice?

The Supporting People programme is premised on a belief that vulnerable people can, with the right support, be enabled to attain or maintain independent tenancies. The same values are also central to the *Valuing People* White Paper (DH, 2001): the words 'rights', 'independence', 'choice' and 'inclusion' summarised its vision for the future of services for people with learning disabilities. *Valuing People* recognised housing, and housing-related support, as central to ensuring that these principles were translated into reality, stating that: "Expanding the range and choice of housing, care and support services is key to giving individuals more choice and control over their lives" (DH, 2001, p 71).

The government endorsed the values at the heart of supported living in its subsequent report on improving the life chances of disabled people (Prime Minister's Strategy Unit, 2005) but positive words and values cannot, by themselves, change lives. This is one reason why Supporting People is of such importance – because it provides a funding stream to help translate values into reality.

Although policy makers are signing up to the core values of supported living, opinions continue to vary widely about *how* services based on the principles of choice, control and independence can be delivered most effectively. This was evident during this research in the way that the different words – 'choice', 'independence' or 'control' – were each favoured by a different group of interviewees when talking about supported living. In each case, a different emphasis and interpretation were given to these words. Although none of the groups of interviewees limited themselves exclusively to a single word to symbolise the most important aspect of supported living, during our analysis of interview transcripts it was evident that different groups had marked tendencies towards different word usage – as shown in Table 2.

Table 2: Which groups emphasised which values?

Value	Dictionary definition	Favoured by
Choice	*Noun.* (1) an act of choosing; the right or ability to choose, (2) a range from which to choose	Support staff
Independent	*Adjective.* (1) free from outside control; not subject to another's authority, (2) not depending on another for livelihood or subsistence	Managers and commissioners (Supporting People teams, social services, housing officers, health commissioners)
Control	*Verb.* (1) have control or command of; in control – able to direct a situation, person or activity	Tenants

These differences in language use are not just semantics. They appear indicative of the values closest to different groups of our interviewees and of the groups' role within the structure of supported living services. One way of examining and interpreting these differences is by relating the language used to the different relationships that each group of interviewees had to the tenants.

'Choice'

Support staff, for example, frequently used the word 'choice' when talking about tenants' lives. This might be a reflection of the role that such staff play in supporting tenants' everyday decision making. Support staff may not, therefore, generally think of tenants as 'independent': they are individuals who need support to make choices, and as such are *not* independent. However, 'choice' often failed to transcend daily routine, as we will see later in this chapter.

'Independence'

By contrast, managers and commissioners habitually referred to the work that they did as promoting 'independence'. They appeared to view independence as the most important value within supported living, because it was the antithesis of the institutionalised services that they were attempting to move away from. These interviewees did not focus on 'choice' because they do not deal with the everyday.

However, in a very real sense these were the people who made many important choices on behalf of people with learning disabilities including where someone would live, who they would live with and how much support they would get, as we will see later. To put it another way, these were the people who denied people with learning disabilities the chance to make choices. They should have been only too aware that tenants very often lacked choice in relation to the bigger picture of their lives. Their preference for focusing on independence may therefore be interpreted as a way of sidestepping this important issue. Equally, however, their preference for promoting independence may have been driven by financial pressures, since it was linked to the need to 'move people on' in order to free up resources for others – something we will return to in the final chapter.

'Control'

Interestingly, tenants themselves tended to use the word 'control' – or, more accurately, the phrase 'being in control' – to describe what they felt to be the most important aspect of supported living for them. This may have been a reflection of the fact that, because they received support from a staff team, most tenants did not regard themselves as 'independent', but were nevertheless determined to be in control of the support they needed. Tenants did refer at times to 'choosing' (for example choosing what to eat for tea). However, tenants' use of the words 'choice' and 'choosing' tended to be linked to specific acts, and was often in response to a direct question from the interviewer (for example 'Did you choose what you want to eat?') rather than cropping up in response to more general discussion of their lives.

Having choices and being in control

Interview responses from both tenants and direct support staff often emphasised the extent to which tenants had choices and were in control of their own lives. In these respects, supported living was frequently contrasted favourably to residential care services in which, it was argued, residents had little by way of choice or control. However, it was also evident, particularly from interviews with managers and commissioners of supported living services, that tenants' choices were often limited to the everyday and the mundane. When it came to 'bigger' choices, such as where or with whom to live, other factors, including Supporting People eligibility criteria (see Chapter 1), financial limitations (see Chapter 4) and management decisions with service provider organisations, could all at times work to limit the control available to tenants.

Limitations of choice

Support staff frequently described tenants' lives as involving a considerable amount of 'choice'. Phrases such as "I think they have choices", "It's their choice" and "Everyone here gets a choice" cropped up regularly. It was interesting to note, however, that the staff who asserted the mantra of choice most vociferously were often those who worked in services based on shared tenancies and/or deregistered care homes – where, in fact, choices were most often limited to the immediate and the everyday.

An arguably more accurate assessment of the extent to which tenants were able to make choices was offered by a support worker who provided support to people living in individual tenancies:

> 'I think what to wear, what to eat, what activities they do are all quite, are there for them. But where they live and who they live with, they're not always consulted, and who supports them, no, that would not necessarily be their choice.'

When pushed, other staff also recognised that tenants' choices were sometimes limited in respect of important aspects of their lives, most often in relation to:

- where to live;
- who to live with;
- who to receive support from.

Where to live

All interviewees acknowledged that choice was severely limited in this area of people's lives. This was often ascribed to a general lack of social housing or the even more limited availability of social housing that met particular needs – such as for clustered individual flats or level access. One support worker summed up the limitation on housing with the comment that, "They were asked if they wanted to go into supported living, but this house was already selected for them".

The majority of tenants felt that they had made the decision to move into supported living. There was, however, some confusion over the role of 'helpers' – such as social workers – in the decision-making process. There was a marked tendency, particularly among tenants who had previously lived in residential care, to say, initially, that a social worker had decided they would move and then, later in the conversation, assert that the choice to move had been their own. Those tenants who had previously lived in their family home had often moved into their new home at a time that was not of their own choosing – for example, following the death of a parent or, in one case, after statutory services became aware that their parents were abusing them.

Who to live with

Choosing who to live with was an issue that only directly affected people in shared tenancies, although people in KeyRing's 'living support networks' or other forms of clustered individual tenancies would also be affected by this to a lesser extent. Care managers, or other professionals not involved in direct support work, played a significant part in determining who would live with whom – in some cases, this amounted to an almost complete lack of choice for tenants. However, there were also some heartening examples of services that tried hard to give tenants a real say in who they lived with. A manager in one service described how, during the planned closure of a local hostel and transition of its residents to supported living services, social workers and independent advocates had worked with the individuals concerned to find out who among them wanted to share new homes. They applied the same principles of choice once the supported living service was up and running, which included giving existing tenants a role in deciding who else would move in.

Who to receive support from

We did not come across any examples of services in which the decision about who to receive support from was an entirely free choice for tenants. According to the managers we interviewed, many supported living services actively involved tenants in the process of staff recruitment. Sometimes this was as part of the formal interview. In other organisations tenants were able to meet and question prospective staff informally. Those services that had yet to involve tenants in staff recruitment were in the minority, and almost all of these avowed their intention to introduce tenant involvement in this area as soon as possible.

In an organisation of any size it is clearly not possible for *all* tenants to be involved in the selection of *every* member of staff who might eventually be involved in their support. In fact, only four of the tenants we spoke to had themselves ever taken part in the recruitment of prospective staff. In an immediate sense, therefore, most tenants had no choice in who was employed to support them. Equally, services did not typically allow tenants to choose which member of staff would provide the support they needed on a day-to-day basis. Indeed, some services explicitly did not want tenants to choose which member of staff supported them, in order to prevent overdependence on their favourite staff member and to retain the sometimes blurred distinction between staff member and friend. This was true for people in both shared and individual tenancies. Although most tenants appeared broadly content with the staff who did come into their homes, the majority understandably described the service manager as being in control of deciding who would support them.

Support staff (but *never* the tenants themselves) occasionally voiced the opinion that choice was unduly emphasised: "A lot of them don't want too much choice. It's too much of a worry, isn't it?" More commonly, however, understandings of choice appeared to be limited by low expectations. There was a tendency, among support staff and other professionals alike, to see choice in comparative terms. And the favoured reference point against which interviewees measured the degree of choice available to tenants, was not ordinary people leading ordinary lives in the UK, but people with learning disabilities living in institutional care. By this measure, supported living services are always going to appear as though they offer a high degree of choice.

Comparing choice and control in supported living and residential care

Some supported living schemes were streets ahead of residential care in terms of the choice and control that tenants could exercise, while others, especially shared tenancies, did not appear to result in significant benefits.

Choice and control were more evident where people had individual tenancies. However, as we have seen, this was partly dependent on the ability of tenants to do things independently. Overall, it seemed that the most able tenants gained most from individual tenancies, while less able individuals, particularly those who were unable to leave their home safely without someone accompanying them, had more access to choices if they lived in shared tenancies, where there was a greater availability of staff support.

People who had moved into supported living from residential care or hostel accommodation cited clear reasons for preferring supported living. These reasons sometimes involved having gained a greater degree of choice and control within the home, for example being able to choose what to watch on television:

'It's better than residential. Staff there were always telling me off, telling me not to watch telly. I can watch it here; I'm in charge of my own remote control; in residential, staff had the remote control.'

For some, the degree of choice available to them now was due in part simply to living with fewer people. For example, three men who now shared a home on a farm said, "There were too many other people at the residential. We couldn't choose what we wanted".

The views of staff about residential care tended to echo those of the tenants, with most strongly believing that supported living was a better option. Support staff described their role as being to 'support', 'teach' and 'empower' and often emphasised how their aim was to enable independence and eventually reduce support:

'Staff are advisers rather than in charge; empowering and teaching – with the aim to eventually reduce the support provided.'

'Once the tenants get that confidence and that ability we can actually pull out a bit more, and they'll have that bit more freedom.'

'We don't do things for them, we just suggest that they get on with it.'

'It's a growing process and a reducing of support.'

Notably, these comments were very much in line with what Supporting People teams hoped would happen, that is, enabling support to existing tenants to be reduced and the funding released to support new tenants.

By contrast, support staff described life for residents of registered care homes as lacking privacy; lacking one-to-one time with staff; living within a predetermined routine and "living under the net of an institution". They were not, however, always speaking from direct personal experience, and much of the negativity about residential care seemed to be based on a belief that this necessarily involved large groups of people living together and not being treated as individuals.

Interestingly, there was a much broader range of opinions among staff who had previously worked in residential care. Ex-residential staff, who were now supporting tenants in *individual* tenancies, typically found their new role radically different from their previous posts:

> 'I actually worked as a domestic for social services and it was a residential [home] so everything was done for them. So then, when I come in here to work, I expected to be doing everything. And I come in and it was like "What am I supposed to do?" 'Cos I was absolutely amazed. I just presumed that we would have to do everything for them, and you don't. And I've also noticed, as well, these in here are a lot happier than what they are in a residential [home].'

Some of the staff who worked in *shared* tenancy services, however, found the differences less notable. One commented that, "There's not much difference in my job really" and another described a routine in a previous residential care home that, but for the greater number of residents, differed little in comparison with that in some shared tenancies:

> 'As I say, to me, there's not much difference because, even in residential, we supported them. You know, they all had their own cleaning day so we'd support them to strip their beds and hoover the floor. We'd give them polish to polish. Like after dinner, there'd be eight of them, one of them would clear the table, one of them would help take the dishes to the dishwasher. You know, one of them would hoover the floor. So we still taught them [to be] independent in the residential home.'

Staff values, skills and attitudes

According to the comments of most tenants and support staff, the key difference between supported living and residential care, in terms of *outcomes* for tenants, was the extent to which the former provided support that promoted choice and independence and gave tenants more control of their lives. Particularly in relation to shared tenancies, this key differentiating factor was clearly related to the values, skills and attitudes of the support staff employed.

Both support staff and managers in the support provider organisations who employed them, spoke of the need for staff in supported living services to be committed to fulfilling an enabling role. This was not always an easy role to fulfil.

Staff who had previously worked in residential care often described finding their new role more challenging than their old one. In particular, it was difficult for some to learn how to 'stand back' and, sometimes, let tenants learn from their own mistakes. One person who had not worked in residential care services described colleagues as needing "to hold back and remember that they [tenants] are adults and can do it themselves". Another recognised the immense challenge presented by the need to change working practices, commenting:

'If you worked in a residential setting for, say, 16 years, and you go to supported [sic] people, it's a big, drastic change. So you need to be able to cope with the difference and learn the different skills that you do need to put into place.'

Managers of several supported living services deliberately aimed to recruit staff who did *not* have a background in residential care. They said that this was because such individuals had 'no preconceived idea' of what working with people with learning disabilities entailed. They believed that inexperienced staff were able to take on board the ethos of supporting living "far more quickly than the ones coming from residential care" and, as a consequence, tended to make better support workers.

Whatever the background of newly employed staff, it was agreed by service managers that effective induction training was crucial – and that this needed to focus as much, if not more, on the *values* associated with Supporting People as it did on practical aspects of providing support. The importance of appropriate training for staff was demonstrated by interviews with staff in deregistered care homes. It was these people who were most likely to believe that there was no difference between working in residential care and working in supported living services. The inevitable difficulties of transition – from one kind of service to another – were not helped by the fact that many of these staff had not received sufficient information about Supporting People *or about supported living*, or any training in how their new role as a supporter would differ from their previous role as a care worker.

Keys as symbols of control

For many tenants, one of the most potent symbols of the difference between residential care and a supported living tenancy was the fact that they held the key to their own front door; tenants in shared tenancies often also had keys for their own, lockable, bedroom doors. However, ownership of house keys and room keys was not always the sole preserve of tenants.

Almost every supported living service had some system whereby a spare set of keys was held, to be used in the event that a tenant lost their own keys or that staff could gain entry to the property, or room, in case of an emergency. But, in some cases, the use of keys by support staff went much further than this. As with so many other issues relating to choice and control, staff practices in shared tenancies and – in particular – deregistered settings often left most to be desired. In these services, we found key systems that were more typical of residential care, such as 'handover' of master keys from one shift to the next, and staff having their own set of front door keys, which they routinely used to enter tenants' homes. By contrast, all staff who worked with tenants in individual tenancies were absolutely clear that they would always knock and wait to gain entry to someone's home – the use of spare keys here was strictly limited to emergencies, where there was cause to believe that a tenant needed help, but was unable to answer the door.

Independence, risk and duty of care

As we indicated earlier in this chapter (see Table 2), commissioners, in contrast to support staff, spoke less about 'choice' and more about their desire to promote 'independence' for people with learning disabilities. (By commissioners we mean people who controlled budgets and purchased services, including Supporting People officers, care managers and health/joint commissioners of specialist learning disability services.) There was not an absolute distinction here between the two groups of interviewees: many support staff made comments to the effect that they saw their work as enabling or promoting independence. However, service managers and commissioners seemed to think about independence in a rather different way.

Many commissioners, in particular, saw independence as being both a goal in itself for individual tenants and a means to an end in terms of the possibilities it offered for reducing staff input and freeing up resources. They appeared to be largely untroubled by philosophical musings about the meaning of 'independence' and whether it was a state that anyone – with or without a learning disability – could realistically achieve or would, indeed, wish to achieve.

Independence or interdependence?

However, two service provider organisations we visited *did* have a more philosophical take on the issue of independence. Specifically, both KeyRing and the intentional community explicitly rejected the idea that independence should be the main outcome of supported living. It was not that either of these two very different organisations were *opposed* to people learning new skills or being encouraged to do things for themselves – far from it. But they both – in very different ways – saw the promotion of *interdependence* as being their goal. The KeyRing model, with its focus on creating networks of support between tenants living within a prescribed geographical area and actively helping tenants to develop other 'natural' supports within their local community, has already been outlined in the previous chapter.

The intentional community (a working farm with livestock and crops) differed radically from all of the other services visited in that it did not seek geographical or social integration with the surrounding area. Within the boundaries of the community, however, life for everyone – with and without learning disabilities – was based on holistic integration. Everybody was treated as an equal. Everybody actively contributed to the work that needed to be done in order to make the community as self-sufficient as possible. The non-disabled community member to whom we spoke described how the community operated in the following terms:

> 'Each one of us contributes according to ability to the whole, which expresses itself [in] that nobody works for money. And I cannot stress how incredibly important that little detail is. But we work because our work is a sense of self-fulfilment, of worth, usefulness, of being needed. [...] Now, what is so lovely: if you're in a team it doesn't really, in the end, matter how big or small your contribution has been, you're part of a team and you identify with it.'

These sentiments were backed up by community members with learning disabilities: both the individuals who were formally interviewed and others whom we met and observed during our visit.

This particular intentional community undoubtedly provided a wonderful home for all community members, but it did this through the creation of a very specific environment that might not suit everyone. (It is, moreover, important to make a distinction between this type of community and the kind of so-called 'village communities' created on the site of some long-stay hospitals. The latter employ paid staff, with a result that they are effectively organised as a cluster of shared tenancies set apart from the wider community. We did not visit any such village communities in the course of this research.)

Overall, the 'mainstream' services funded by Supporting People had a focus on promoting independence rather than interdependence. It was believed (or hoped) that any increased independence on the part of individuals could reduce the cost of service provision and hence free up funding for new tenants or developments. In addition, independence was often discussed by professionals in relation to risk-taking, which in turn was linked to the concept of 'duty of care'.

Independence and risk

Independence was intrinsically linked with the concept of risk in the minds of virtually all of our interviewees: that is, risk taking, risk assessment and the minimisation of risk. This was true for both tenants and all groups of professionals, although understandings of, and attitudes towards, risk showed some noticeable variations. As with other aspects of supported living, there was a tendency for the risks associated with supported living to be compared and contrasted with those associated with residential care. Based on the findings of this research, we would suggest that a number of points of comparison do exist between these two ways of delivering services (see Table 3), each of which will be discussed in turn.

Table 3: Supported living versus residential care: a comparison of perceived risks

Supported living	Residential care
Risk that activities undertaken could lead to negative outcomes, eg injury, ill-health, social embarrassment	Risk that activities *not* undertaken will limit the development of practical, social and relationship skills
Tenants empowered to take control of their own lives, including complaining if their support is substandard	Residents often unaware of their rights and may be unaware of the possibility of complaining
Risk of bullying and abuse from members of the local community	Risk that the local community will not know that bullying and abuse is occurring behind closed doors
Risk of abuse from members of staff	Risk of abuse from members of staff
Regulatory framework provided by inspection of services by Supporting People: varies from area to area	Regulatory framework provided by Commission for Social Care Inspection (CSCI): national standards

The right to take risks

Both managers and commissioners of supported living services were very clear in asserting that, as adults, all tenants had a right to choose for themselves how they wished to live their lives. Furthermore, it was acknowledged that for people with learning disabilities in supported living, execution of this right necessarily involved a degree of risk-taking. Phrases such as "It's everybody's right to take risks, that's how we learn", "It's their choice" and "We can only advise" cropped up repeatedly, with the general mood summed up by the following quote:

> 'They've got a right to make choices and they've got a right to make mistakes. You know, at the end of the day, it's like all of us: we don't always make the right decisions.' (Manager of support provider organisation)

It would be wrong, however, to give the impression that these interviewees thought that such principles were simple to put into practice. Service managers, especially, stressed the need for tenants to make informed choices and spoke of the emotional impact that allowing tenants to take risks could have on frontline staff. Despite these caveats, however, the bottom line remained the same:

> 'The staff are encouraged to talk about how they feel about that. But, also, to acknowledge that actually, well, somebody knows the risk but they're still going to do it and, at the end of the day, they're living in their own home and you ain't going to be able to stop them.' (Manager of support provider organisation)

On both a philosophical and practical level, it was the potential for taking risks that distinguished supported living from residential care.

Nevertheless, despite the uncompromisingly pro-independence statements from service managers, it was evident from speaking to support workers that there was sometimes reluctance on their part to encourage those types of independence that were regarded as high-risk. This was partly due to worries that, if a tenant came to harm in any way, the organisation would have failed in its duty of care. There was often a feeling among support staff that there was 'a very fine line' between meeting their duty of care on the one hand (and, in doing so, running the risk of limiting individuals' independence) and allowing individuals to take risks (which could be perceived as being negligent in their duty of care) on the other.

A crucial way of helping support staff through this minefield was the systematic use of risk assessment. Service managers emphasised that risk assessment could and should be used 'to enable people to do things', rather than as a bureaucratic way of saying 'no'. They repeatedly emphasised too that, in order to be of any practical use, risk assessment had to be both particular (to an individual person and an individual activity) and dynamic (monitored and amended on a regular basis, as skills and confidence grew).

Several interviewees also acknowledged that part of the reason for using risk assessment was because "at one level there's needing to protect ourselves". This, in turn, could lead to a situation in which support staff's awareness of risk tended to focus on immediate danger (for example road safety or bullying and abuse from strangers) rather than the damaging potential outcomes of long-term behaviours (for example poor diet or lack of regular exercise). This was perhaps inevitable, since it was the more immediate dangers which support staff sometimes had to respond to. One man, for example, insisted that he wished to use public transport by himself. He did so, but got lost and was missing for 10 hours. Similarly, in another service, a tenant fell down the stairs after an evening drinking in the pub and ended up in hospital.

Tenants' experiences of danger and abuse

Although staff were concerned – to a greater or lesser extent – with all aspects of risk, tenants themselves were largely concerned with their personal safety. To be more specific, they were concerned with the potential danger posed to them by other people, rather than any danger they might cause to themselves. Only one tenant – a man with high physical support needs – said that he was safe because he "didn't cook meals" by himself. When other tenants were asked about feeling safe or unsafe, all of them responded by talking about whether or not they had been the victims of various types of bullying, harassment, abuse, interpersonal violence or crime.

The majority of tenants, whether in individual or shared tenancies, said that they felt safe within their own homes. In two of the clustered tenancies, however, tenants were concerned about home security – they were particularly worried about the failure of other tenants (with or without learning disabilities) to lock shared communal entrances. In one of the clustered tenancies (in a council tower block), tenants had at times been scared to walk along the communal stairs and landings because "there are lots of druggies", although staff reported that the police had been involved and this problem had been largely overcome.

A significant proportion of the people we spoke to described incidents in which they had been the victims of crime and abuse. One group of young men who shared a home described how:

> 'We've already had stuff nicked. We let people in. We knew them and they stole stuff.'

Examples such as this, which basically involved members of the public abusing the trust and friendship of people with learning disabilities, were not uncommon. In another service, in a different part of the country, staff recounted how they had temporarily taken control of a tenant's finances (by removing a bank card from his possession) after he was 'befriended' by a group of people in the local pub, who then persuaded him to take large sums of money out of his account and give it to them. The police had been involved, but the money was not recovered.

Stories of bullying and harassment from neighbours and passers-by were recounted even more frequently. These included instances of street robbery; being followed by groups of kids; being beaten up on the way home from an evening out; being verbally abused in the street; and being harassed by a neighbour banging on the windows and ringing the doorbell late at night. As a consequence of such incidents, many tenants described feeling unsafe when they left the house – particularly in the evenings. Some spoke of how such bullying and harassment had led them to curtail their social activities. Some did not go out at all in the evenings, while others would leave the pub early to avoid the possibility of violence at closing time.

Adult protection issues

In addition to the stories we heard directly from tenants, we were also told of other serious instances of crime and victimisation – usually in interviews with senior social services staff, because their professional remit included responsibility for adult protection. A typical statement was that "We've had a number of issues around adult protection for people who are living in their own home with limited support", which would then be followed by a variety of, often harrowing, stories. They gave us accounts of tenants becoming embroiled in drugs and prostitution; numerous examples of financial exploitation; and one horrific case in which a woman living alone had been raped by a door-to-door salesman. None of these more extreme examples of abuse related to the tenants we met. They were, nonetheless, the kinds of scenario that haunted professionals with responsibility for the protection of vulnerable adults.

All managers and commissioners were, to a greater or lesser extent, aware of the recent national roll-out of policy guidance aimed at helping to protect vulnerable adults, including people with learning disabilities, from abuse (DH, 2000; ADSS, 2005). However, their active engagement in the protection agenda did not mean that they were opposed to risk-taking:

'We do a lot of things on personal safety and protection of vulnerable adults. But they're as safe there as they would be anywhere because we have the systems in place. You know? And they've got a right to make mistakes.' (Social services manager)

Both tenants and support staff spoke only of actual or potential abuse, bullying and harassment that people with learning disabilities might be at risk of experiencing from members of the general public. But in addition to abuse from this source, managers and commissioners were also aware of the possibility that abuse could be perpetrated by support staff. Living alone, particularly for people with higher support needs or limited verbal communication, could be regarded by some as placing tenants at greater risk of abuse by staff, since they would typically work alone, unobserved by others. Rigorous recruitment processes and effective staff training were seen as important ways of minimising such risks:

'And, of course, you do all the usual checks and references and police checks. But there's always some people who can slip through. And then it's about monitoring them. And other staff, you know, being trained [to spot] any signs of abuse, as well.' (Manager of support provider organisation)

Inculcating support staff with the right values and having a clear focus on providing a high-quality service were similarly regarded as protective measures:

'We have another provider [not interviewed for this research] where we've got some concerns about the quality of the service. And, again, just looking at the overall service in terms of adult protection, we're addressing some concerns where it's quite clear that the staff don't have the same attitude towards the service users or respect the fact that it is their own house. I won't say more than that because we are, you know, investigating this under our adult protection procedures. But, quite clearly, the staff don't regard the service users' house as their property and their domain.' (Social services manager)

It was also recognised as crucial that managers and commissioners monitored services effectively. Although just how this monitoring could best be achieved was a point of contention, as we shall see in the next section.

Regulation of services

One of the most significant aspects of Supporting People is that the services it funds for people with learning disabilities are not, by definition, registered care homes. In practical terms, this means that the services are not subject to the national regulatory framework and compulsory inspection regime of the Commission for Social Care Inspection (CSCI). Instead, services funded by Supporting People monies are inspected by members of the local Supporting People team. As a result, inspections of supported living services are *not* governed by national standards, although they are all loosely based on the Supporting People Quality Assessment Framework (QAF) developed by the ODPM (ODPM, 2004b).

Some critics have suggested that CSCI inspections tend to focus on bureaucratic matters, such as record keeping, rather than the quality of life of service users. However, it was evident that a number of our interviewees had found CSCI to be a valuable resource in supporting the maintenance of service quality in their provision for people with learning disabilities. At least one organisation had found inspection reports to be a useful way of getting hold of extra resources, explaining that once CSCI had declared a certain input to be necessary then it had "got to be provided", and this was a trump card when negotiating with commissioners for funding. Another had decided against the deregistration of some of their services because "as much as we argue with them, they're [the CSCI are] a massive support to us; it's very clear where you stand with them". This appeared to be in contrast to the same organisation's experiences with the local Supporting People team – who were not unhelpful, but were "still trying to find their own feet" and were not yet fully up to speed with their implementation of QAF at the time the research was conducted.

In areas where Supporting People teams had better-developed local QAFs, most service providers appeared to find little difference in the effectiveness of Supporting People inspections as compared to those carried out by CSCI. Indeed, several interviewees who provided supported living services in more than one local authority area commented that the QAF was no more or less consistent in its approach than the supposedly national standards of CSCI. Overall, it appeared that the fact that independent monitoring of service quality took place was more important than which organisation undertook the inspection visits.

Where supported living services were being provided for less able (and therefore, perhaps, potentially more vulnerable) people, these could be subject to both CSCI and QAF inspections, since if an individual's need for support exceeded the Supporting People maximum hours or included 'ineligible' tasks, the extra support had to be funded from social services community care budgets as domiciliary care. In such cases, support providers were obliged to register with CSCI as a domiciliary care agency and so would become subject to their regulations too, which meant – as the manager of one support provider organisation put it – both "more regulation and more protection for service users".

Involvement in strategic planning

A final area where tenants might be expected to be demonstrating some participation and control is in the strategic decision making and planning of the housing and support services that so directly affect their lives. The participation of people with learning disabilities is heavily encouraged in *Valuing People* (DH, 2001). In similar fashion, guidance from the ODPM to administering authorities on producing their five-year strategies for Supporting People stipulated that these should be developed with input from meetings "inclusive of all relevant partners" (ODPM, 2004d). But the findings of our analysis of five-year strategic plans (see the Appendix) showed limited evidence of involving people with learning disabilities in the strategic decisions for the future of the Supporting People programme. This was evident in both the way in which strategies were produced and which groups of tenants were included in plans for the future.

Thus, it was disappointing to find that very few indeed – a mere 5% – had produced an accessible version of the strategies, with easy words and pictures, so that people with learning disabilities might have an opportunity to understand some aspects of the plans being made about their future services.

Table 4 (overleaf) shows the extent to which Supporting People teams had involved various stakeholder groups in the development of their five-year strategies.

Given the high proportion of Supporting People money that was being spent on supporting people with learning disabilities, it is disappointing to see from Table 4 that less than half of all administering authorities had ensured that people with learning disabilities were involved in, or consulted about, the development of their strategic plans. It is uncertain whether this reflects unwillingness on the part of Supporting People teams to engage with tenants with a learning disability, or simply a lack of knowledge about how best to do so.

Table 4: Which groups of stakeholders were consulted in drawing up strategies?

	% of strategies
Social services	100
Local authority housing departments	99
Voluntary and independent sector housing support providers	92
Tenants (other than people with learning disabilities)	90
Primary care trusts	88
Housing associations/registered social landlords	55
People with learning disabilities	45

Encouraging good practice

Based on the findings reported in this chapter we offer the following good practice checklists:

Good practice checklist 5: Choice and control

- In which aspects of their lives can and do tenants supported by this agency make their own choices?
  - Are these areas in which tenants can make informed choices?
  - If not, what might they need to know to assist their decision making?
- What support is available to help tenants make important and/or difficult choices?
  - Self-advocacy?
  - Independent advocacy?
  - Family and friends?
  - Care managers/social workers?
  - Accessible information?
- What aspects of tenants' lives in your area or agency remain under the control of others?
- How could the balance be shifted towards giving tenants greater choice in important aspects of their lives, such as where and with whom they live?
- How do you ensure that the views of tenants with learning disabilities are fed into the strategic planning of Supporting People services?

Good practice checklist 6: Risk

(1) Consider the various types of risk to which individuals may be exposed:
  - physical risks
    - external/environmental (eg risk of falling down stairs)
    - internal/biological (eg risk of heart disease from poor diet)
  - social risks
    - emotional/psychological (eg bullying, harassment)
    - sexual (ie sexual abuse)

- financial risks
  - acts of commission (eg money being stolen or otherwise misused)
  - acts of omission (eg tenants not informed of the benefits to which they may be entitled).

(2) Think about *who* may be at risk as a result of a particular action or inaction:
- tenant himself/herself
- other tenants or neighbours in same building
- support staff
- others living in the local community.

(3) Think about different timescales over which any risk might arise:
- immediate risk (eg fire, as a result of smoking in bed)
- long-term risk (eg damage to health as a result of lack of exercise).

(4) Balance what might happen if an individual decided to take a particular risk *against the consequences of not taking that risk:*
- likelihood of a negative outcome
- seriousness of the possible negative outcome
- duration of the possible negative outcome.

(5) When undertaking risk assessments, remember that such assessments:
- cannot (and should not aim to) eliminate risk
- do not (of themselves) make anything less risky
- should identify *all* dimensions of risk associated with a particular individual or activity
- can and should be used to enable, not prevent, risk-taking
- can provide *evidence* of staff meeting their 'duty of care'.

4

Financial matters

After pilot interviews for the study it became clear that tenants, service providers and service commissioners alike wanted to talk to us about a wide variety of financial matters related to the Supporting People programme.

It was beyond the scope of this study to address the finances of the programme at governmental level – issues like the overall size of the Supporting People pot; the consequences of legacy provision for nationwide equity of access; and the future impact of a national distribution formula. But in this chapter we report the project findings relating to the financial impact of Supporting People on the individuals who receive support and on the support staff and independent organisations who provide it. We also look at the financial issues for support provider organisations in trying to meet the costs of social support for tenants, coping with the financial risk associated with the funding stream and developing new services. Finally, we look at what our analysis of the five-year strategies tells us about how funds have been used in different administering authorities.

Tenants' personal finances

It was commonly believed by commissioners and managers of supported living services alike that one of the many benefits of providing support in this way was that tenants would be better off financially, as compared with living in a residential care home. The truth that emerged from our conversations with tenants was a rather more complex picture of financial losses and gains, based not only on absolute financial truths but also on tenants' perceptions of how much money they received, balanced against what they had to pay for.

The benefits system

A move into supported living from residential care meant an increase in the amount of money flowing through a person's bank account. This is because in residential care residents have all of their needs – for care, support, food, household cleaning products, heating, lighting, rent, Council Tax, water rates, television licence and so on – met centrally, leaving them just a small 'personal allowance' each week with which to purchase clothes, toiletries and other personal effects.

Supported living services are funded very differently. Tenants' support needs are paid for by Supporting People, but they then either claim benefits or work, just like any other adult members of society. This means that tenants in supported living are responsible for paying for *all* of the items listed above. Although Housing Benefit and Council Tax Benefit would cover the rent and Council Tax of people *not* in paid employment, living on Jobseeker's Allowance or Incapacity Benefit does not provide a generous household budget.

The simple system outlined above, however, only represented the financial situation of a fairly small number of tenants in our study. Many were also eligible for Disability Living

Allowance (DLA), a tax-free benefit for people who need help with personal care or who have mobility problems as a result of being physically or mentally disabled. In addition, tenants who were in paid employment and were working for 16 or more hours each week could claim Working Tax Credits. The overall effect of this tax and benefit system was that those tenants who were the most – or least – able, tended to be the better off, because they could either work or were entitled to DLA. Those people who found themselves in the middle of the spectrum – too able to claim DLA but not able to find paid employment – could suffer significant financial hardship. For example, of the tenants we spoke to, one married couple (who were able to work and claim both tax credits and DLA) estimated their monthly income to be in the region of £1,300; and a young man who lived alone, but who received higher rate DLA, had recently purchased new furniture and a widescreen television. By contrast, other tenants, who did not qualify for DLA and were not in work explained how their weekly budget left little cash for social activities once they had paid their bills and purchased food and other household essentials, many making comments such as "I'd like to have more money".

Money as independence

Money was usually regarded by tenants (and often by support staff) as one of the aspects of living independently that was most difficult to handle. While we did meet one or two people who had a strong grasp of their finances, most needed a great deal of support in this area. The newer banking technologies had both helped and hindered tenants' money management. Having benefits paid directly into a bank account and setting up direct debits to pay rent and other regular household bills meant that income and expenses could be maintained with minimal effort. But such systems often meant that tenants had little genuine understanding of their incomes or outgoings and would not be in a position to know if anything was going awry. Moreover, the need to remember pin numbers in order to access cash caused problems for tenants: they were aware that they should keep their number a secret, but often struggled then to remember it.

On a day-to-day level, many tenants had complex systems involving cash tins; various envelopes with sums of money for different activities; savings accounts for the purchase of larger items; and weekly shopping trips supported by staff. A number of people felt that this left them with too little to live on. One man complained that he "daren't ask for any more [money]; staff say I have enough". Another interviewee told us, "I got money in the bank. I don't know how much. They won't tell me in case I want it all."

The difficulty for staff appeared to be that they were sometimes in a position of having to help tenants live on quite tight budgets. Tenants therefore seemed to blame staff, rather than the benefits system, when they could not afford everything they wanted. For some, the transition from residential care was financially difficult – in particular coming to terms with having 'more' money, but not being able to spend this as they pleased. One tenant felt he had less money because he now had "bills to pay". In the following example, a tenant complained about lack of food but appeared to be choosing to spend most of her money on other items or activities:

> 'Tuesdays I get £25: £10 shopping and £15 for me. Fridays I get £35: £20 shopping and £15 spending. Not much money for shopping on Tuesday, should go up a tenner. Never have anything in the fridge, have to make it last. Don't buy much. Only buy Weightwatchers' dinners; get the same things over and over again. Can't find anything else to suit me for the price.'

The tenant quoted above was one of several who said they were either worse off financially or 'about the same' as a consequence of moving out of residential care and into supported living.

Despite the difficulties experienced by some tenants, others did appear to be relatively content with their day-to-day financial situation. Many happily allowed staff to look after their money, trusting that this way they would always have enough to eat and for other activities important to them. Several were being helped to save money on a regular basis, so that they could go on holiday.

This support sometimes, however, appeared to result in provider organisations holding a significant degree of control over tenants' money. In particular, it was notable that (especially in shared tenancies) tenants were required to obtain receipts for any money they spent. These receipts were then handed over to support staff as part of a system of financial audit. It could be argued that this was a sensible precaution against financial abuse. Nevertheless, such systems not only absorbed considerable amounts of staff time, but also inevitably resulted in closer monitoring of tenants' expenditure and hence less financial control for tenants themselves. However, it should be noted that although some tenants appeared to resent the extent to which staff controlled their personal finances, others grudgingly accepted the limits of their financial freedom: "Staff look after my bank and benefit books; I'd spend it otherwise".

Money and social support

The most contentious financial issue for many tenants was the fact that, if they wanted or needed to have staff support to undertake social activities, they had to pay for both themselves and their support worker. This meant, for example, that a tenant might have to pay for staff drinks or meals out: "We go out for a drink with staff, we have to pay for them". Others would have to pay for staff to go with them on their holidays: "Have to pay for them to go to Blackpool. I don't think it's right".

Staff paying from their own pocket

While it was understandable that tenants on a low budget might resent having to pay for staff in this way, the alternative seemed to be just as unfair on staff. Some organisations had systems whereby staff could claim small amounts of expenses if they escorted a tenant out for a meal or to the pub, but this rarely if ever reflected the actual costs involved. For example, one organisation allowed staff to claim back a maximum of £3 for a meal. But, in practice, as one of them pointed out to us, "Where can you get a meal for £3, or even £5, now? So, in actual fact, if you wanted a meal you'd be paying for it out of your own pocket".

One solution was simply for staff not to eat with tenants when they went out, but this could create problems of its own:

> 'I supported one tenant who got most irate because I wouldn't eat. And he actually shouted at me in the restaurant. I was most embarrassed. I promised, faithfully, that I would eat with him next time. But, I mean, what I usually try and do is actually fund my own, which actually becomes quite expensive.' (Support worker)

The pressure on staff to subsidise services in this way was often acute, and could result in considerable expense for them. One member of staff described paying for drinks or food four or five times each week; another said that they often spent £20 or more each week this way. Given the low salaries typically associated with support work, it does not seem reasonable to expect staff to be paying out in this way.

Cash rich but social support poor

The irony was that some tenants, typically individuals in shared tenancies – with household costs minimised by sharing food and splitting bills – and who were entitled to higher rates of DLA, found themselves in a relatively comfortable financial position. However, despite in some cases having significant savings, it was often still difficult for these people to engage in social activities in the way they might wish. One member of staff described how the tenants she supported had plenty of cash, but were often stuck indoors because there was nobody to support them to get involved in social activities, as these did not count as eligible Supporting People tasks:

> 'I honestly believe the service users that I support are very well off financially, which to me seems crazy that they have the money for holidays and for going out, and yet we find it so difficult. The volunteer sector are [sic] really stretched and we find it very difficult to find volunteers. And in theory they have the money to pay for someone to do the things, but we can't find an organisation to do it.'

In essence, she was describing tenants who were 'cash rich' but 'social support poor'. This is a real problem to which Supporting People appears to offer no solution. As the same worker pointed out, staff were, in fact, constantly being encouraged to help tenants find ways to spend their money "so that their benefits aren't penalised" (that is, to spend money in order to ensure that bank account balances remained below the permitted threshold for claiming benefits). Yet there was no way for tenants to purchase what they often wanted the most – support to spend extra time out of the house, engaged in meaningful social activities.

Financial issues for support provider organisations

The interviews for this research were conducted at a time of great uncertainty regarding the future size of the Supporting People budget at both national and local level. Service provider organisations were concerned about the effect that any tightening of eligibility criteria or cuts in hours of support available to tenants might have on their ability to continue to provide high-quality services. For example, on the day we visited one shared tenancy service it had just heard that, as a result of a recent local review of Supporting People expenditure, the four tenants would together be losing 35 hours of support each week; the equivalent of one full-time member of staff. The likelihood of organisations facing such severe cutbacks depended very much on whether their Supporting People team was making changes to their lists of eligible tasks and/or reducing the maximum number of support hours they were willing to fund per person per week (see Chapter 1) – or not.

The future of Supporting People services looked very different in different administering authority areas. This depended in part on the extent of legacy provision (services that had originally been funded from THB), with areas with large amounts of high-cost legacy provision likely to face year-on-year budget cuts as a consequence of the new national distribution formula (a way of determining the distribution of Supporting People funding based on selected socioeconomic indicators, introduced in 2004 following the Matrix Research & Consultancy [2004] report). The intention of the ODPM was that this formula would result in a more equitable distribution of Supporting People monies across the country. But it was clear from the areas we visited that cuts were falling not only in those authorities with large amounts of legacy provision or unnecessarily high costs, but also those whose socioeconomic profile did not match the selected indicators – for example, rural areas where costs were higher due to the diseconomies of providing services to geographically dispersed populations.

Moreover, in those authorities that had particularly large amounts of legacy provision, the potential reductions in funding as a consequence of the distribution formula were massive and unexpected:

> 'I don't think anybody could have predicted the implications of the distribution formula which would see us possibly losing up to 45% of our grant.' (Supporting People officer)

There were in addition a number of other, perhaps less well publicised, financial issues confronting service provider organisations, which could have lasting consequences for supported living services. Each of these will now be addressed in turn.

Community care savings: tenants' loss

Support provider organisations, in common with many of the tenants whom they supported, were keen to draw attention to the difficulties associated with trying to put social support in place, which we have referred to earlier in this report. Interviewees from many organisations spoke of how Supporting People eligibility criteria militated against tenants accessing the social support they needed to become active and engaged members of their local community. Although this problem affected all organisations equally (or, at least, all of those in the same administering authority, since rules varied between areas) it was felt most keenly by those who had already been providing supported living services before the introduction of first THB and then Supporting People. These supported living services had previously been funded from local authority community care budgets, and had typically either received funds specifically in order to support social activities, or had managed to provide such support from within their overall funding. When Supporting People came along, these services were automatically transferred (some would say 'cost-shunted', see Introduction) out of community care and into the new funding stream, with social support costs now excluded. The effect of this was to force providers to withdraw from the social support that they had previously included automatically as a central part of their support for tenants. There was considerable frustration at this change in eligibility under the new funding regime. As the manager of one such service put it: "It would have been reasonable to say 'These things won't be eligible'. It's not reasonable to go, a few years on, and say, 'Oh, no, actually that's not now'. You know?"

Some organisations were, in the short term, trying to continue meeting the social needs of tenants by cross-subsidising the associated support costs from other budgets, but were acutely aware that such practices could not continue indefinitely.

Shifting the balance of financial risk

The impact of withdrawing funding for social support falls mainly on tenants, of course, but Supporting People also heralded other financial changes that support provider organisations feared could have a direct impact on their own survival. The biggest of these was the change in contracting arrangements, from the block contracts of community care to individual contracts under Supporting People.

Essentially, under the old system of block contracting, community care commissioners would block-buy services: for example, they might choose to purchase four beds in a registered care home. If, for any reason, a vacancy arose (due perhaps to a resident dying or moving on), the provider organisation would still receive funding while a new resident for the empty place was identified. By contrast, under Supporting People, funding would immediately cease once a tenant moved out, including if they became ill and were admitted to hospital. Supporting People did, in some circumstances, pay 10% of the costs of 'voids' (empty bedspaces), but despite this token gesture interviewees complained bitterly about the impact voids could have on their ability to operate on a sound financial footing. Some organisations even went so far as to say that they would prefer to develop residential care homes in the future, rather than supported living services: "We'd have to think twice before developing any more of those projects because you can't afford to, you know, 'cos if you have a void you get no income" (Manager of support provider organisation).

Individualised contracts, by contrast, should mean a complete separation of bricks-and-mortar housing from housing-related support is possible, so tenants can theoretically choose to change their support provider at will, while still remaining in the same home. However, we found that in practice almost no tenants were aware of these rights and many lived in accommodation that was, in fact, owned by the same organisation as that which provided their support. The main effect of the changes to contracting arrangements was simply, therefore, to shift the costs of empty bedspaces onto support provider organisations.

Although the rationale for individual contracts sounded positive and was presented as enabling services to be tailor-made for each individual, this issue seemed to have the potential to scupper future service developments. Interestingly, several interviewees – including people both from support provider organisations and in commissioning roles – believed that the idea of breaking the link between bricks-and-mortar housing and housing-related support for people with learning disabilities was a mistake. They argued that, in fact, the two needs were intrinsically connected and were, therefore, best met together.

Funding new services

Several provider organisations were concerned not only about whether they themselves might invest in the development of supported living services in the future, but whether any other organisations would be willing to take the financial risk involved. As well as the financial risks posed by 'voids', there were worries over the year-on-year across-the-board cuts planned by many administering authorities in response to the reduced government funding for Supporting People. In some cases, organisations believed they had more to fear from this kind of top-slicing approach than they did from the complete closure of services. This was because many had fixed future costs, including annual salary increments for staff.

One manager described how:

> 'We're going from interim contracts to steady state contracts, you know, they can put three-year contracts in place. And they're going to be fixed-cost contracts, there's going to be no uplifts in those. Now, that's fine as long as we can put the third-year prices in our budgets! But I don't think we're going to be able to. You know, for us, we could probably go at a profit in the first year and make the loss on the third. But we can't … we can't run a three-year contract on the first year's prices. We can't do it.'

Another simply said:

> 'Providers are not going to enter into contracts that, you know, are not going to give you an uplift each year. [...] No business person, no matter if they're not-for-profit, is going to go into something where they're going to end up with a loss.'

Chief among the worries of managers of provider organisations was how to balance the value of the programme for developing supported living with their need for financial stability. The main concern was that Supporting People is an insecure source of funding – a theme that cropped up in almost every interview:

> 'I would hope that there will be more money coming through. But I don't think that ... I don't think that's the case.'

> 'Our biggest fear is that they're going to reduce the service to save money.'

Those providers who only supported tenants with a learning disability were also very concerned about the possibility that this was a service user group that would be targeted for cutbacks as Supporting People eligibility criteria were tightened. However, several were quietly confident that – having used Supporting People monies to prove the effectiveness of supported living as a framework for service delivery – they were now returning to a position where new developments were attracting alternative funding:

> 'Where we're talking about a new network, they're talking about that being funded by social services.' (Manager of KeyRing scheme)

> 'What's happened, very quickly, is that local authorities have come to us and said, "We want a particular scheme developed. There's no Supporting People money, we'll fund it out of social services community care budgets". So we're actually, already, starting to get back to different funding streams. And it may be that health might then start to put funding in. So, yes, we are being funded through other means, along with Supporting People, for our learning disability services.' (Housing Association officer)

Local variations in funding and future plans

Two years after the launch of the Supporting People programme in 2003, every administering authority in England was required to submit a five-year strategy to the ODPM, outlining the future of the Supporting People programme in their area. In our analysis of these five-year strategies (see the Appendix), it was noticeable that not all administering authorities were willing, or able, to provide a financial breakdown of their Supporting People expenditure or to state the number of individuals who were receiving support. For example, almost one-fifth of strategies (18%) failed to state their total Supporting People budget and 17% did not say how many people were being supported.

Where information was available, it did provide strong evidence to suggest that a significant proportion of Supporting People money was being used to support people with learning disabilities and that the average cost of support packages was higher for people with learning disabilities than for other tenant groups.

Where figures were available, the number of individuals receiving support ranged from 402 to 19,013 per administering authority. Annual costs per person varied from £778 to £6,393. The number of people with learning disabilities who were receiving Supporting People services ranged from 24 to 1,144 in different authorities. Annual costs per person with a learning disability varied between £4,374 and £27,442 in different areas, with an average of £12,685. In percentage terms this means that while only 0.66-8.15% of those who were receiving Supporting People services had a learning disability, between 5% and 54% of the available money was being spent on them.

These numbers were distorted to a certain extent by the inclusion in the figures provided by some (but not all) authorities of alarm services for older people. Alarm services typically cost a few pounds per person per annum and involve only an emergency response service rather than any regular support. By counting every person with an alarm as an individual in receipt of services, the average cost of support per person is reduced, making the contrast in costs between tenants with a learning disability and others appear even greater.

Despite the distorting effect of including alarm systems, however, support packages for people with learning disabilities are higher cost, on average, than those for other groups of tenants.

As shown in Figure 1, there was considerable variation in the proportion of the Supporting People budget allocated to people with learning disabilities by different administering authorities. Six per cent of authorities spent between 5% and 10% of their overall Supporting People budget on support for people with learning disabilities; a further 37% of authorities spent up to 20% of their budget on this group. But it is authorities with an

Figure 1: Percentage of administering authorities' budgets spent on tenants with a learning disability

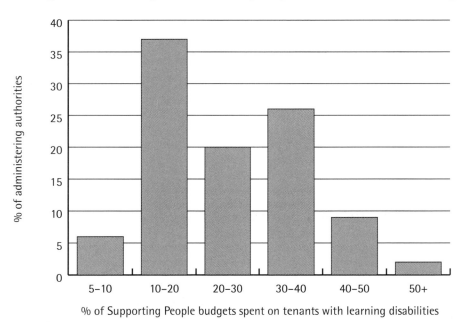

% of Supporting People budgets spent on tenants with learning disabilities

extremely high proportion of Supporting People budgets being spent on people with learning disabilities that may be particularly vulnerable to future service cuts: the 9% of authorities which spent 40-50% of their budgets on learning disability and the 2% who spent over half their entire Supporting People budgets on this group.

The variation in average annual costs, and the proportion of budgets allocated to learning disability, did not relate in any consistent way to socio-demographic factors such as regional population density or relative economic prosperity. In fact, one or two London boroughs, where one might have expected to see high average costs as a result of the higher costs of staff wages, had rather low average expenditures and high average expenditures were found in several relatively economically deprived areas of northern England. It is likely, therefore, that cost variations reflect differences in the support needs of tenants with learning disabilities, with some administering authorities having inherited many more high-intensity/high-cost support packages as a result of legacy provision from THB.

How were funds used?

In those administering authorities that were now facing the most severe budgetary reductions, managers of support provider organisations, managers and commissioners from health and social services, housing officers and members of Supporting People teams all agreed that their strategic thinking during early implementation of the programme had to some extent been flawed. Housing officers in particular were critical of the way in which – to their way of thinking – a fund designed to pay for housing-related support had been diverted for other purposes:

> 'I don't think that the local authority has used the opportunity of Supporting People creatively enough. I think they've used it to sort of – I don't know if I want to turn that [that is, the researcher's tape recorder] off now, actually – create savings in their own budgets.'

> 'I think local authorities have used Supporting People to deliver their statutory services rather than use general fund money, if that's fair to say. And, maybe, more of that Supporting People money ought to be used to pick up those people who've got lower … you know, don't hit the threshold and wouldn't normally go into a statutory threshold.'

This was a point which some in social services were willing to concede, with one interviewee describing how Supporting People was initially regarded as "an opportunity to grab, really: get the loot!" The same person, however, went on to acknowledge that with the benefit of hindsight, this had not been such a good tactical manoeuvre:

> 'Since it's been, you know, looked at more closely it's evident that there isn't actually enough to go round and they're looking at cuts now, as well. […] And, obviously, there'll be an impact on social services, if the cuts are made, in the budget. And I don't know how we'll actually manage that.' (Social services manager/commissioner)

Encouraging good practice

Based on the findings reported in this chapter we offer the following good practice checklists:

Good practice checklist 7: Tenants' finances

(1) Are all tenants receiving *all* of the benefits to which they are entitled?
   (a) Whose job is it to do this?
   (b) How often do you check whether tenants' circumstances and entitlements have changed?

(2) How are tenants supported to not only live within their financial means, but also to understand where their money comes from and where it is spent?
   (a) Do tenants understand the amounts they pay for rent, household bills, Council Tax, television licence, etc?
   (b) What training do staff receive in relation to supporting tenants to budget effectively (in particular, in how to explain financial matters to tenants)?

(3) To what extent are tenants in control of their own finances?
   (a) Do they have to get receipts for all monies spent? If so, why?
   (b) Are they given support to save for more costly items or activities, should they wish to do so?
   (c) Has the possibility of employment been fully explored – including explaining the financial implications?

(4) How are tenants' social support costs met?
   (a) Who pays the out-of-pocket expenses of support staff?
   (b) How might tenants who are 'cash rich' but 'social support poor' be enabled to purchase social support hours?

Good practice checklist 8: Organisational finances/commissioning considerations

(1) How are the cost of 'voids' shared between the commissioning agency and the support provider organisation?
(2) Do contracts allow for year-on-year cost uplifts that reflect the true cost of wage inflation and increases in non-staff costs?
(3) What impact is the current balance of financial risk having on the willingness of support providers to develop new services?
(4) How is the commissioning of housing-related support services linked, at a strategic level, with the development of bricks-and-mortar housing?

5

Concluding comments

The aim of this research project was to explore the impact that the Supporting People programme was having on housing and support for people with learning disabilities in the four administering authorities that took part in this study. We conclude our report with some reflections on our findings, outlining some of the positive outcomes that can be attributed to Supporting People funding, but also some notes of caution about some of the unintended consequences of the programme.

First steps to independence

On an individual level, the lives of some people with learning disabilities have been transformed by the support they have received via this funding stream. For them, Supporting People monies made it possible to take control of their lives for the first time, enabling them to make choices about everyday activities and to achieve a degree of independence that had previously been denied them. In a very real sense, Supporting People provided the money with which to make a reality of some of the aspirations of *Valuing People* (DH, 2001) – a White Paper that had arguably achieved a great deal in terms of changing attitudes, but less in terms of creating new services.

The tenants we interviewed – many of whom had been highly critical about some of their previous homes – spoke in warm and positive terms about their present circumstances. When asked where they might like to live in the future, most replied that they were happy where they were. In general it seemed to us that this group of people were no more dissatisfied with their current homes than might be expected in any random sample of the population.

Only one tenant was particularly negative about his future: a young man with mild learning difficulties but severe physical impairments, who felt that there was "nowhere else to live". He was also one of the tenants who had expressed feelings of loneliness. He felt that he needed more hours of support than were available, both to ensure his physical safety and to enable him to better access community activities. However, he was the only person we came across with such major reservations about their supported living service.

Many managers and commissioners were keen to point to the benefits that had accrued from the Supporting People programme. This included a significant expansion in the availability of supported living services for people with learning disabilities, and with it the potential to access a far wider range of housing options:

> 'Supporting People will fund floating support – it actively seeks to promote a vision of the future where there is less emphasis on specialist housing units and more people are able to take up independent individual tenancies with the local authority, a registered social landlord or within the private rented sector.' (Supporting People officer)

Other benefits identified by interviewees included a stronger relationship between local authority housing and social services departments. One social services manager described how this had created housing options for people with learning disabilities from general council stock. Another pointed to ways in which his housing department had responded positively once they became aware of the demand for housing from people with learning disabilities:

> 'To now see housing application forms developed in accessible format, I think, is a very direct result of all these developments and the sort of options that we've got now that we didn't have in the past.'

It was hoped by many that access to general housing might prove to be a breakthrough for meeting the housing needs of people with learning disabilities. However, it should be pointed out that in many authorities – particularly in the south and east of England – council housing stocks are very limited. And, even in areas where housing was relatively available, concern remained about where future funding for support would come from. In addition, there was particular anxiety about those people with learning disabilities who had not secured funding in the early stages of Supporting People, but were now seeking financial support – including young people wishing to leave home for the first time.

Support for living?

Despite the many positive aspects of the Supporting People programme, its implementation did also have some less encouraging outcomes. In particular we noted the extent to which our interviewees repeatedly raised concerns about the difficulty of accessing funding to support social activities, under Supporting People. These difficulties were sometimes overcome or circumvented in a variety of creative ways. But the fact that Supporting People funding is not designed to meet these support needs created problems for people with learning disabilities – and the commissioners, providers and staff involved in facilitating their support – if they wanted to become a part of their local community, like other people, and in line with the aspirations of *Valuing People*.

Housing-related support is undoubtedly important in enabling people to attain and maintain independent tenancies, but where this type of support is provided in isolation the consequences for people with learning disabilities may be that they remain excluded from their local communities, lonely and vulnerable to abuse. To genuinely receive 'support for living' many people with learning disabilities who receive Supporting People funding need both housing-related support *and* social support. Social support must therefore either be made available from other sources or the rules preventing Supporting People money being spent in this way must be relaxed.

Looking ahead

Our analysis of future service developments (as outlined in authorities' five-year Supporting People strategies) suggests the likelihood of both good and bad news for people with learning disabilities. Unless there is a significant increase in the provision of jointly funded support and care packages (with money from social services and/or health as well as Supporting People), it seems likely that there will be little foreseeable increase in the availability of supported living as an option for people with high support needs in the future. On the other hand, there may be better provision for individuals with low support needs, many of whom may have not previously received support of any kind, because they have not met the threshold criteria for community care services.

Although many authorities were hoping to increase the *number* of people with learning disabilities to whom they provided support, it was clear that the only way in which this goal could be achieved would be by reducing the maximum costs of individual packages . of support – in practice, this could mean limiting Supporting People funding to those with less severe learning disabilities. In this sense, it can be argued that Supporting People has served to further highlight the general underfunding of services for people with learning disabilities (ADSS, 2005).

The instability of funding through Supporting People was also a major concern for those charged with planning and providing services. Overall, 79% of administering authorities said that they were expecting reductions in their future Supporting People budget, with 39% explicitly stating that they were aiming to *reduce* expenditure on support for people with learning disabilities in the future.

As for the type of supported living arrangements, there is evidence in the five-year strategies that administering authorities are keen to see the expansion of both home ownership and private renting as options for people with learning disabilities. More of these new homes are likely to be individual rather than shared; and there will be an overall movement away from accommodation-based support towards less cost-intensive support options, including floating support, KeyRing schemes and low-level support services.

Supporting People officers who we interviewed believed that in the future they would be under pressure to provide support to many more *individual* tenancies. However, the assumption that people with learning disabilities would want to move on from shared tenancies to individual tenancies was not borne out by our findings. Relatively small numbers of tenants wished to move from shared tenancies to individual flats. Unlike other groups of Supporting People service users, people with learning disabilities are likely to require ongoing support for many years. Other researchers who have undertaken detailed population-based research into the housing and support needs of people with learning disabilities (McGlaughlin et al, 2001, 2002) have found a huge desire for greater housing choice, and fuller involvement in decision making, but only a small proportion of people (less than 3%) wanting to live alone, with a further 9.5% expressing a preference for 'own accommodation in shared unit' (McGlaughlin et al, 2002).

But is it supported living?

Despite the upbeat individual stories and the much-needed injection of cash into services for people with learning disabilities, the impact of Supporting People in other ways has been more ambiguous. As a result of the rapid expansion of self-styled 'supported living' schemes we sometimes encountered an alarming disparity between the realities of the services we visited and the principles of effective supported living outlined the Introduction (see Paradigm, 2002).

Measured against these principles, many of the schemes based on shared tenancies failed to come near the required standards. This is *not* to imply that these schemes were offering a poor-quality service, but simply to suggest that what they were providing *was not supported living*. Tenants may have had legal tenancy agreements, but many were still not afforded the right to take control of the most important aspects of their lives – such as where and with whom to live, or from whom they wished to receive support.

The findings of this study make it difficult to acclaim Supporting People as an unequivocal gain for people with learning disabilities, since the sudden availability of this funding stream appears to have had the effect of *increasing* the availability of supported living at the expense of *decreasing* its meaning, and associated benefits. Moreover, the funding of services that do not appear to adhere to supported living principles has left services for people with learning disabilities particularly vulnerable to budget cuts. In its review of Supporting People services the CSCI (2006, para 2.4) commented that "substantial growth in opportunities for people with learning disabilities has led to some inappropriate use of the Supporting People grant and some schemes may not be sustainable".

In the understandable rush to secure Supporting People funding, services were sometimes established that could not immediately meet all of the provisos of fully fledged supported living. But some managers and commissioners we spoke to appeared not to be aware of the need for such services to change significantly in order to truly become what they were already proclaiming themselves to be. There is, therefore, a danger that, if these schemes continue to claim the title of 'supported living' and receive Supporting People monies, people with learning disabilities living in them will lose the regulatory protection afforded by registered care homes and the financial protection afforded by statutory funding *without* gaining the choice and independence that should be an integral part of supported living. It is vital that managers and commissioners within learning disability services work to ensure that the increased availability of supported living, through the availability of Supporting People monies, is both meaningful and sustainable. People with learning disabilities deserve nothing less.

Glossary

Accommodation-based support: support provided by a team of staff working in a single building or group of dwellings.

Administering authorities: a generic term for the various types of local government authorities responsible for administering Supporting People monies.

Assured tenancy: a legally binding form of tenancy that provides some degree of security of tenure for the tenant.

Cash-limited budget: a budget with a fixed amount of money each year (as distinct from one which is determined by demand, as is the case with some benefits).

Commissioners: those people in statutory services who control budgets and purchase services, including Supporting People officers, care managers and health/joint commissioners of specialist learning disability services.

Floating support: support from staff who visit individuals in their own home, but are not based there.

Individual tenancy: a single individual holds the tenancy rights to the whole of a self-contained property.

Intentional community: where people with learning disabilities live alongside other (non-disabled) people as equals in an intentionally created community with shared goals.

Legacy provision: services that were initially funded under the Transitional Housing Benefit system, before being transferred to Supporting People on 1 April 2003.

Mixed packages of care and support: where support is provided by pooling funding from more than one agency's budget in order to meet the different needs of an individual.

National distribution formula: a way of determining the distribution of Supporting People funding based on selected socioeconomic indicators, introduced in 2004.

Providers: shorthand for provider organisations and/or the senior staff managing them (as distinct from staff involved in giving day-to-day support to tenants).

Shared tenancy: two or more people who are not related and do not share an intimate relationship, occupying the same property. Typically, individuals in a shared tenancy would have their own bedroom but share a communal kitchen and living area.

Sheltered accommodation: housing designed as individual units for older or disabled people but with a shared warden and (sometimes) facilities for communal use or social activities.

Statutory duty: a statutory entitlement – or legal right (under the 1948 National Assistance Act) – to certain support services, because of the individual's level of care needs, funded either by social services or the NHS.

Supported living: a model of providing housing and support where people's housing needs are assessed, and met, separately from their needs for support. The aim is to enable people to be in control of their own lives as far as possible, including where, how and with whom they live.

Supporting People programme: a government funding initiative aiming to offer improved ways of providing housing-related support to people who need help to retain their housing tenancies and attain or maintain independence. It went live on 1 April 2003.

Support staff: frontline staff directly responsible for supporting tenants on a day-to-day basis.

Transitional Housing Benefit (THB): the term used for payments made under the shadow Supporting People programme, which operated for two years before the system went live on 1 April 2003. During this period central government encouraged local providers to access the new funding stream; there were no specified limits to the amount of support that could be provided for an individual service user.

Voids: empty spaces in a shared property, or an empty individual tenancy.

References

ADSS (Association of Directors of Social Services) (2005) *Safeguarding Adults*, London: ADSS.

ADSS (2006) *Pressures on Learning Disability Services: The Case for Review by Government of Current Funding*, London: ADSS.

Arblaster, L., Conway, J., Foreman, A. and Hawtin, M. (1996) *Asking the Impossible? Interagency Working to Address the Housing, Health and Social Care Needs of People in Ordinary Housing*, Bristol: The Policy Press.

Arblaster, L., Conway, J., Foreman, A. and Hawtin, M. (1998) *Achieving the Impossible: Interagency Collaboration to Address the Housing, Health and Social Care Needs of People able to Live in Ordinary Housing*, Bristol: The Policy Press.

ASL (Association for Supported Living) (2004) *Provisional List of the Attributes of Supported Living Schemes*, Witney, Oxon: ASL, www.associationsupportedliving.org/aboutUs.php

Atkinson, D. (1997) *Forgotten Lives: Exploring the History of Learning Disability*, Kidderminster: BILD.

Beyer, S., Grove, B., Schneider, J., Simons, K., Williams, V., Heyman, A., Swift, P. and Krijnen-Kemp, E. (2004) *Working Lives: The Role of Day Centres in Supporting People with Learning Disabilities into Employment*, London: Department for Work and Pensions.

CSCI (Commission for Social Care Inspection) (2006) *Supporting People – Promoting Independence: Lessons from Inspections*, London: CSCI.

DETR (2001) *Supporting People: Policy into Practice*, London: DETR.

DH (Department of Health) (1999) *Facing the Facts: Services for People with Learning Disabilities: A Policy Impact Study of Social Care and Health Services*, London: DH.

DH (2000) *No Secrets: Guidance on Developing and Implementing Multi-Agency Policies and Procedures to Protect Vulnerable Adults from Abuse*, London: DH.

DH (2001) *Valuing People: A New Strategy for Learning Disability for the 21st Century*, Cm 5086, London: The Stationery Office.

DWP (Department for Work and Pensions) (2006) *Improving Work Opportunities for People with a Learning Disability: Report of a Working Group on Learning Disabilities and Employment*, Leeds: Corporate Document Services.

Emerson, E., Malam, S., Davies, I. and Spencer, K. (2005) *Adults with Learning Difficulties in England 2003/04*, London: DH.

Fyson, R. and Ward, L. (2004) *Making 'Valuing People' Work: Strategies for Change in Services for People with Learning Disabilities*, Bristol: The Policy Press.

Gillinson, S., Green, H. and Miller, P. (2005) *Independent Living: The Right to be Equal Citizens*, London: Demos.

Gorfin, L. and McGlaughlin, A. (2003) 'Housing for adults with a learning disability: "I want to choose, but they won't listen"', *Housing, Care & Support*, no 6, pp 4-8.

Griffiths, S. (2000) *Supporting People all the Way: An overview of the Supporting People Programme*, York: Joseph Rowntree Foundation.

Guardian, The (2003) *Cunning shunts: shadow over social services as Supporting People budget balloons*, 22 October, http://society.guardian.co.uk/offdiary/story/0,,1099066,00.html

HM Government (2005) *The Government's Annual Report on Learning Disability 2005. Valuing People: Making Things Better*, Cm 6700, London: The Stationery Office.

Hunter, M. (2006) 'Flip side of private provision', *Community Care*, 3-9 August, pp 26-7.

Kinsella, P. (1993) *Supported Living: A New Paradigm?*, Manchester: National Development Team.

Lewis, J. and Glennerster, H. (1996) *Implementing the New Community Care*, Buckingham: Open University Press.

McGlaughlin, A., Gorfin, L. and Saul, C. (2001) *Assessment of Housing and Support Needs for Adults with a Learning Disability in Nottingham City: Final Report*, Nottingham: Nottingham Trent University, Department of Social Sciences.

McGlaughlin, A., Gorfin, L. and Saul, C. (2002) *Assessment of Housing and Support Needs for Adults with a Learning Disability in South Nottinghamshire (Nottingham Health Authority District): Final Report*, Nottingham: Nottingham Trent University, Department of Social Sciences.

Matrix Research & Consultancy (2004) *Briefing Paper: Proposals for Developing the 'Supporting People' Distribution Formula*, London: ODPM.

Means, R. and Smith, H. (1994) *Community Care: Policy and Practice*, London: Macmillan.

ODPM (Office of the Deputy Prime Minister) (2004a) *What is Supporting People?*, London: ODPM.

ODPM (2004b) *Quality Assessment Framework – Core Service Objectives*, www.spkweb.org.uk

ODPM (2004c) *Supporting People: Shadow Strategy Analysis 2002 2003*, London: ODPM.

ODPM (2004d) *The Essential Guide to Developing the 5 Year Supporting People Strategy v1.0*, www.spkweb.org.uk

ODPM (2004e) *Supporting People User Involvement Guide*, London: ODPM.

ODPM (2005) *Creating Sustainable Communities: Supporting Independence. Consultation on a Strategy for the Supporting People Programme*, London: ODPM.

ODPM (2006) *Help us to Make Supporting People even Better*, London: ODPM.

Paradigm (2002) *Reach – Standards in Supported Living*, Liverpool: Paradigm.

Prime Minister's Strategy Unit (2005) *Improving the Life Chances of Disabled People*, London: Prime Minister's Strategy Unit.

Robson Rhodes (2004) *Review of the 'Supporting People' Programme: Independent Report*, London: ODPM.

Rolph, S., Atkinson, D., Nind, M. and Welshman, J. (2005) *Witnesses to Change: Families, Learning Difficulties and History*, Kidderminster: BILD.

Simons, K. (1995) *My Home, My Life: Innovative Approaches to Housing and Support for People with Learning Disabilities*, London: Values into Action.

Simons, K. (1998) *Living Support Networks: An Evaluation of the Services Provided by KeyRing*, Brighton: Pavilion Publishing.

Simons, K. (2000) *Pushing Open the Door: 'Housing Options' – the Impact of a Housing and Support Advisory Service*, Bristol: The Policy Press.

Simons, K. (2001) *Developing Housing & Support Options: The Changing Regulatory Context*, www.bris.ac.uk/Depts/NorahFry/Strategy/index.htm

Simons, K. and Ward, L. (1997) *A Foot in the Door: The Early Years of Supported Living in the UK*, Manchester: National Development Team.

Skills for People (2004) *Skills for Support*, Newcastle: Skills for People.

SOLD (Shared Ownership for People with Learning Disabilities) Information on housing is available on the Valuing People Support Team website: http://valuingpeople.gov.uk/dynamic/valuingpeople153.jsp?highlight=Housing Advance Housing and Support have made 'The SOLD booklet' to help people understand what 'Shared Ownership' is and if its right for you – find out more by ringing 01993 709221 or email homeownership@advanceuk.org or look on the web at: www.advanceuk.org/pages/process_content.asp?idno=378&sub=68&top=1122&portal=housing

Valuing People Support Team (2005) *Valuing People: The Story so Far*, London: DH.

Watson, L., Tarpey, M., Alexander, K. and Humphreys, C. (2003), *Supporting People: Real Change? Planning Housing and Support for Marginal groups*, York: Joseph Rowntree Foundation/York Publishing Services.

A considerable amount of data about the provision of Supporting People services is now published by the government at www.spkweb.org.uk/Subjects/Statistics/

Appendix: Methods

Interviews

Interviews were carried out with a variety of people, as shown in Table A1.

Table A1: Number of interviews with different respondents

	Number of interviews
Person with a learning disability	31
Support staff	11
Provider organisation – manager	10
Supporting People team	4
Social services (care) manager	5
Health service commissioner	2
Local authority housing officer	2
Housing association officer	1

Interviews with tenants were conducted using an approach that can best be described as abbreviated life story work. Essentially, the interview process consisted of the researcher sitting down with one or more tenant and completing a 'life audit'. Interviewees started off by taking a photograph of themselves (and, if they wished, of their home) and then talked through the major areas of their lives – their living situation (past and present), friends, family, daily activities, finances, support staff and so on. These areas were based on areas identified as important in *Reach – Standards for Supported Living* (Paradigm, 2002); the *Skills for Support* information pack, which was developed by a group of self-advocates in Newcastle (Skills for People, 2004); and the *Provisional List of the Attributes of Supported Living Schemes* developed by the Association for Supported Living (ASL, 2004).

All of the tenants who participated in this research were able to communicate verbally; where two interviewees spoke only Bengali, an interpreter, who worked as an advocate for the two individuals concerned, spoke to the tenants on the researchers' behalf. The original intention was to interview tenants individually, but in the event many preferred to be interviewed in pairs. Paired interviews often elicited a greater amount of information, particularly from tenants who were less confident about the interview process, than attempts at individual interviews. In many cases it also enabled interviewees to support one another in remembering events or expressing likes and dislikes.

Following the interview, the information from each tenant was used to create an individual life story book. Each book included any photos that the interviewee had chosen to take alongside an accessible (easy words and pictures) account of what they had told us. These books were returned to tenants as a way of showing them how we had collated their information. They were also used by the research team as the basis for evaluating the information provided by tenants.

Interviews with other respondents listed in Table A1 (for example, support staff and managers of provider organisations, members of Supporting People teams, care managers, commissioners and other officers) were all tape recorded and transcribed in full prior to analysis. The analysis focused on both identifying shared areas of concern (for example, Supporting People officers and other professionals alike were very concerned about the definition of 'supported housing') and drawing out examples of best practice that we feel may be of use to others.

Analysis of local authority five-year plans

Using the database on the government's Supporting People website (www.spkweb.org.uk) we wrote to the Supporting People team in each of the 150 English administering authorities requesting a copy of their five-year Supporting People plan. The response was very good, with between 70% and 100% of strategies being collected in each region, and an overall collection rate of 77%. A full breakdown of strategy collection by region is provided in Table A2.

Table A2: Breakdown of strategy collection by region

Region	Number of administering authorities	Number of strategies collected	% of strategies collected
East of England	10	8	80
East Midlands	9	9	100
London	33	23	70
North East	12	9	75
North West	22	16	73
South East	19	16	84
South West	16	12	75
West Midlands	14	12	86
Yorkshire & the Humber	15	11	73
Total	150	116	77

The five-year plans that we received were read through by a member of the research team. From each plan, a number of factual details were extracted for quantitative analysis, including various financial indicators; evidence (if present) of the eligibility criteria used by that authority; details of plans for the development of future services for people with learning disabilities; the involvement (if any) of service user groups in the plan's development; and explicit linkages to other policy agendas, such as *Valuing People*. In addition, notes were made regarding the overall quality of the plan, its accessibility to people with learning disabilities and to the general public, and the likely impact of the plan on provision of services to people with learning disabilities.

Review of the literature

It was not the intention of this project to provide a comprehensive review of the literature about supported housing for people with learning disabilities. However, information regarding the Supporting People programme published by both the ODPM (2004c, 2005, 2006) and information regarding the implementation of the *Valuing People* White Paper published by the Valuing People Support Team (2005) were regularly reviewed throughout the project in order to cross-reference the two policies.